Growth Mindset Ninja for Teens
A Ninja Life Hacks Guide

This book is dedicated to my sons - Mikey, Kobe, and Jojo.

Also by Mary Nhin:

Resilient Ninja | Business Ninja | Emotions Ninja for Teens | Growth Mindset Ninja for Teens | Leadership Ninja for Teens | Self-Management Ninja for Teens | Self-Awareness Ninja for Teens | Social Awareness Ninja for Teens | Decision-MakingNinja for Teens | Relationship Ninja for Teens | Money Ninja for Teens | Angry Ninja | Inventor Ninja | Positive Ninja | Lazy Ninja | Helpful Ninja | Grumpy Ninja | Earth Ninja | Kind Ninja | Perfect Ninja | Anxious Ninja | Money Ninja | Gritty Ninja | Dishonest Ninja | Shy Ninja | Unplugged Ninja | Diversity Ninja | Inclusive Ninja | Masked Ninja | Grateful Ninja | Hangry Ninja | Focused Ninja | Calm Ninja | Brave Ninja | Worry Ninja | Funny Ninja | Patient Ninja | Organized Ninja | Communication Ninja | Stressed Ninja | Smart Ninja | Hopeful Ninja | Confident Ninja | Zen Ninja | Goal-setting | Lonely Ninja | Self-Disciplined Ninja | Motivated Ninja | Sad Ninja | Impulsive Ninja | Feelings Ninja | Creative Ninja | Forgetful Ninja | Nervous Ninja | Emotionally Intelligent Ninja | Growth Mindset Ninja | Jealous Ninja | Frustrated Ninja | Memory Ninja | Listening Ninja | Innovative Ninja | Supportive Ninja | Love Ninja | Humble Ninja | Quiet Ninja | Compassionate Ninja | Sharing Ninja | Caring Ninja | Curious Ninja | Hard-working Ninja | Investments | Problem-Solving Ninja | Integrity Ninja | Disappointed Ninja | eNinja | Healthy Ninja | Adaptable Ninja | Respectful Ninja | Flexible Thinking Ninja | Entrepreneur Ninja | Accountable Ninja | Consent Ninja | Negative Ninja | Sensory Ninja | Tired Ninja | Social Ninja | Neurodivergent Ninja | Happy Ninja | Visionary Ninja | Passionate Ninja | Honest Ninja | Authentic Ninja | Loyal Ninja | Debate Ninja | Collaborative Ninja | Distracted Ninja | Embarrassed Ninja | Negotiator Ninja | Cooperative Ninja | Furious Ninja | Scared Ninja | I Love You, Little Ninja | Gritty Ninja and the St. Patrick's Day Race | Kind Ninja and the Easter Egg Hunt | I Love You, Mom - Earth Ninja | I Love You, Dad - Grumpy Ninja | Patient Ninja's Halloween | Grateful Ninja's Thanksgiving | Ninja Life Hacks Christmas | Ninjas Know the CBT Triangle | Ninjas Go to the Dentist | Ninjas Go to Europe | Ninja Go Camping | Ninjas Go to the Library | Ninjas Go Through a Ninja Warrior Obstacle Course | Ninjas Go to a Party | Ninjas Go to Space | Ninjas Go to Work | Ninjas Go to School | Ninja Life Hacks Numbers | Ninja Life Hacks ABCs of Feelings | Ninja Life Hacks Shapes | Ninja Life Hacks Colors | Ninja Life Hacks Body Parts | Ninja Life Hacks Animals | Ninja Life Hacks Opposites | Ninja Life Hacks Weather | Unplugged Ninja in Vietnam | Kind Ninja Builds a Buddy Bench | Magical Mistake Machine | Lunar New Year | Happy Birthday Ninja | Ninja's New Year | Chef Ninja | Engineer Ninja | Teacher Ninja | Doctor Ninja | Firefighter Ninja | Police Officer Ninja | President Ninja | Coding Ninja | Neurologist Ninja | Amelia Earhart | Steve Jobs | Elon Musk | Indra Nooyi | Anne Frank | Serena Williams | Albert Einstein | Mae Jemison | Frida Kahlo | Michael Jordan | Jane Goodall | Helen Keller | Muhammad Ali | The Wright Brothers | Kobe Bryant | Rosa Parks | Ray Kroc | Martin Luther King, Jr. | Michelle Obama | Sara Blakely | Barack Obama | Walt Disney | Peggy Cherng | David Bowie | Mia Hamm | Sam Walton | Tiger Woods | Jackie Robinson | Mother Teresa | Harriet Tubman | Chloe Kim | Neil Armstrong | Ella Fitzgerald | Stevie Wonder | Maya Angelou | Wilma Rudolph | Lionel Messi | Cristiano Ronaldo | Sophie Cruz | Taylor Swift | Sonia Gandhi | Never Ever Marry a Mermaid | Never Ever Lick a Llama | Never Ever Upset a Unicorn | Never Ever Massage a Moose | Never Ever Dance with Dracula | Never Ever Tickle a Turkey | Never Ever Race a Reindeer

Growth Mindset Ninja for Teens
A Ninja Life Hacks Guide

by Mary Nhin

Growth Mindset Ninja for Teens: A Ninja Life Hacks Guide
© 2025 Mary Nhin | Ninja Life Hacks
All rights reserved.

No part of this book may be reproduced, distributed, or transmitted in any form or by any means, including photocopying, recording, or other electronic or mechanical methods, without the prior written permission of the publisher, except in the case of brief quotations embodied in critical reviews and certain other noncommercial uses permitted by copyright law.

For permission requests, please contact the publisher at:
Grow Grit Press LLC
info@ninjalifehacks.tv

First Edition: 2025
Paperback ISBN: 979-8-89614-073-3
Hardcover ISBN: 979-8-89614-075-7
eBook ISBN: 979-8-89614-074-0

Published by:
Grow Grit Press LLC

ninjalifehacks.tv

Disclaimer: The information provided in this book is based on the author's personal experiences and research. It is intended for educational and informational purposes only. The author and publisher make no guarantees of success or improvement from applying the strategies outlined in this book. Readers are encouraged to consult professionals before making health, financial, legal, or business decisions. Some stories in this book are inspired by real events or composite experiences from friends, students, etc. They're meant to illustrate typical teen challenges.

Printed in the United States of America.

TABLE OF CONTENTS

Foreword – By Dr. David Li, Adolescent Development Specialist & Mindset Coach	8
Author's Note – A Personal Message from the Author	13
Introduction – The Power of a Growth Mindset: Why Every Teen Can Benefit	14
1. Perfectionism – Taming Your Inner Perfectionist	17
2. Growth Mindset – Embracing the Power of "Yet"	29
3. Embarrassment – Using S.H.I.N.E. to Conquer Awkward Moments	41
4. Flexible Thinking – Bending the Rules (in a Good Way)	53
5. Fear – The L.I.O.N. Method for Facing Fears	65
6. Grit – The Four Cs for Perseverance	77
7. Fury – C.A.L.M. the Volcano	91
8. Adaptability – Flow Like Water When Plans Change	101
9. Negativity – Emotional Bank Accounts and Trust	115
10. Authenticity – Living by the Four Ls	127
Final Thoughts – Your Ongoing Journey to Confidence, Resilience, and a True Growth Mindset	139
Ninja Moves Glossary	143
Help and Support Resources	148
Books & Resources Mentioned in This Book	154
About the Author	157

FOREWORD

In my years of working with teens, I've witnessed firsthand the incredible power of a growth mindset. From the student who once believed they'd never pass algebra to the young athlete convinced a single lost game meant they weren't "good enough," so many young people stop believing in their potential the moment they hit a roadblock. The truth is, those early roadblocks are where real development begins, if you know how to push past them.

That's why this book, *Growth Mindset Ninja for Teens: A Ninja Life Hacks Guide*, is so timely and essential. Readers learn that mistakes aren't catastrophes; they're stepping stones toward something greater. Each chapter addresses a universal challenge, like tackling perfectionism, facing fears, or building resilience, and distills it into easy-to-remember strategies. These tactics are both practical and empowering, helping you navigate daily life with a spirit of curiosity, flexibility, and optimism.

I've seen countless teens transform from self-doubt and frustration to confidence and courage once they realize they can reshape their thinking. Growth isn't a magic trick you stumble across; it's a skill you practice, day by day. And practice is exactly what these ninja-themed lessons encourage. Instead of scolding you for perceived flaws or lecturing you about "positive thinking," this book invites you to experiment, try new approaches, and view each challenge as a chance to learn.

If there's one message I hope you take from this book, it's that your mind is far more malleable than you might think. The ninjas will be your guides, but you'll always be the hero of your own story. By applying the strategies in these chapters, you'll discover that every "failure" has a lesson tucked inside, every obstacle has an alternate route around it, and every uncertainty can become an opportunity.

I'm delighted to introduce *Growth Mindset Ninja for Teens: A Ninja Life Hacks Guide* to you. May these pages spark your determination, ignite your curiosity, and remind you that your potential is limitless, just waiting to be unlocked, one creative strategy at a time.

—Dr. David Li
Adolescent Development Specialist & Mindset Coach

A HEARTFELT THANK YOU

Writing this book has been a wild, rewarding, and sometimes chaotic adventure, one that wouldn't have been possible without the incredible people who've supported me every step of the way.

To my family, my husband and children, thank you for being my greatest inspiration and my grounding force. Your love, laughter, and unwavering belief in me have pushed me forward, even when self-doubt tried to creep in. You are my reason, my motivation, and my biggest blessing.

To my parents, who left everything behind to build a better life in America. Your resilience, sacrifice, and work ethic have shaped every part of who I am today. Every dream I chase, every goal I accomplish, it's all because of the values you instilled in me.

To my mentors and business partners, thank you for challenging me, pushing me, and expanding my vision beyond what I ever thought possible. Your wisdom has been invaluable, and I am endlessly grateful for the lessons you've shared.

To my incredible team, the powerhouse individuals who help bring these ideas to life. You are the engine behind every success, the quiet force that keeps everything running smoothly. Your dedication, creativity, and relentless passion do not go unnoticed.

To my Ninja Life Hacks readers, followers, and supporters, both big and small,, whether you've been with me from the beginning or just picked up this book today, your encouragement fuels my passion. Seeing how these stories, lessons, and ideas impact your lives is the greatest reward I could ever ask for.

To my Collective for Children family, thank you for believing in the mission to empower every child with resilience, leadership, and emotional intelligence. Your commitment to making a difference is what drives me every day.

This book is not just mine, it is a product of so many incredible hearts and minds that have influenced, guided, and supported me along the way. I am forever grateful to each and every one of you.

AUTHOR'S NOTE

I've always been intrigued by how ninjas move through obstacles, swiftly, calmly, and with a keen sense of purpose. Maybe it's the discipline they embody, or the way they find unseen paths in plain sight. Either way, they remind me that life's challenges can be approached with strategy, courage, and constant learning.

This book is about you stepping into that kind of mindset. Not because you need to scale rooftops or own a closet full of throwing stars, but because you already show ninja-like qualities in everyday life: problem-solving under pressure, finding creative solutions, and learning from every misstep.

As you read, you'll find tips and ideas to help sharpen those skills. And yes, you'll probably encounter moments that feel awkward or uncertain, but that's part of the process. Much like a ninja re-centers after a stumble, every mistake can be a chance to refine your approach.

My hope is that these pages inspire you to navigate challenges with a little more confidence and curiosity. You don't need flashy moves to be resilient; you just need to be willing to adapt, learn, and try again. Thanks for choosing to spend time with these words, and here's to honing the Growth Mindset Ninja in you, one step at a time.

Onward, ninjas! Let's do this.

- Mary Nhin

INTRODUCTION: THE POWER OF A GROWTH MINDSET

Why Every Teen Can Benefit

Life is full of challenges, some exciting, some frustrating, and some that make you want to throw your hands up and walk away. Whether it's struggling through a tough class, feeling stuck in a skill you can't quite master, or doubting yourself when things don't go as planned, it's easy to think, *Maybe I'm just not good at this* or *I'll never figure it out*. But what if you could rewire your thinking and see those challenges not as stop signs, but as stepping stones?

That's where *Growth Mindset Ninja for Teens* comes in.

This book isn't about magically making problems disappear. It's about shifting how you see them, transforming obstacles into opportunities and mistakes into lessons. A growth mindset is the belief that intelligence, talents, and abilities aren't fixed; they grow with effort, practice, and the right strategies. It's about adding the word yet to every "I can't," reminding yourself that you're always a work in progress.

Inside, you'll meet ninjas who have faced the same struggles you do, whether it's battling perfectionism, handling embarrassment, pushing past fear, or bouncing back from failure. Each chapter breaks down real-life challenges, easy-to-remember strategies, and ninja-tested techniques to help you develop resilience, confidence, and the power to *keep going*. You'll find stories, relatable scenarios, and moments of humor that make the learning process fun and engaging.

So, whether you're crushing goals or just trying to survive a tough school year, this book is here to help you unlock the strongest, smartest, and most unstoppable version of yourself. Because the truth is, your potential is limitless. And the more you embrace a growth mindset, the more you'll realize that *you're capable of more than you ever imagined.*

Let's get started, your ninja training begins now!

1

TAMING YOUR INNER PERFECTIONIST

Imagine you're writing an English essay and you've been on the same paragraph for over an hour, tweaking and re-tweaking every sentence until it practically loses all meaning. Or maybe you've been dying to learn a musical instrument but never sign up for lessons because you can't stand the idea of making those squeaky, off-key beginner sounds. If any of this rings a bell, congratulations, you've met your Inner Perfectionist.

A healthy dash of ambition can be wonderful; it drives you to learn new skills, polish your talents, and take pride in what you do. But when it crosses the line into perfectionism, you're left feeling anxious, burned out, or too scared to even try. Over time, perfectionism can build up a wall of all-or-nothing thinking, convincing you that if you're not immediately amazing, you might as well not bother.

So why does it matter? Because constant perfectionism is like carrying a heavy backpack filled with rocks labeled "fear of failure," "self-doubt," and "overwhelm." Not only does that slow you down, but it also blocks you from celebrating small wins, taking risks, or enjoying the process of learning. A Growth Mindset understands that deep drive to succeed but also wants you to stay sane, and maybe even have a little fun, while chasing your goals.

What Perfectionism Does to Your Brain and Body

Still not convinced it's a big deal? Let's peek under the hood:

- Stress Overload
  - » Perfectionists often live in a pressure cooker. Constantly feeling like you must perform at 110% pushes your body to produce cortisol, the stress hormone, which can disrupt sleep, mood, and even your immune system.
- Overthinking Paralysis
  - » Your brain whirls through every possible worst-case scenario. This mental traffic jam leads to procrastination or bailing on new opportunities for fear you'll "mess up."
- Stifled Creativity
  - Ironically, chasing "perfection" can kill innovation. If you only do what you're already great at, you'll never experiment, play, or color outside the lines, which is where real creativity thrives.

Understanding these impacts is like shining a flashlight on a dark corner. Once you see how perfectionism operates, it's easier to catch yourself spiraling and say, "Hold up, maybe there's a better way."

Different Types of Perfectionism

Believe it or not, perfectionism isn't one-size-fits-all. You might recognize yourself in one (or more) of these:

1. The Check-and-Recheck Overachiever
   - » You rewrite the same text message five times before hitting send.
2. The "All-or-Nothing" Mindset

- » If you're not the best, you feel like a failure. Small mistakes can feel so huge, you'd rather not even start if it can't be "perfect."
3. The People-Pleaser
    - » Your desire for perfection stems from wanting everyone else's approval. You're terrified of letting others down, so you overextend yourself to maintain a spotless record.
4. The Obsessive Tweaker
    - » Whether it's an art project or a social media post, you cannot stop tweaking. You revise, erase, and fiddle endlessly, fearing it's never good enough to share.

Some of these might sound relatable, or maybe you're a combo platter of them all! Regardless, spotting your "type" can help you figure out how to ease up and let yourself be human.

The Sneaky Consequences of Uncontrolled Perfectionism

When perfectionism is in overdrive, it doesn't just affect your report card, it spills into your mental, emotional, and even physical well-being. Here's how:

- Mental Fatigue: Overthinking every detail can be mentally draining, leaving you feeling like you've run a marathon, inside your head.
- Increased Anxiety & Stress: Constantly chasing flawless results cranks up the pressure, spiking your cortisol (the stress hormone). You might have trouble sleeping or feel on edge all the time.
- Procrastination: Ironically, needing things to be perfect can stop you from starting a project at all. Why begin if you can't do it "perfectly" right away?
- Fear of Failure: Trying something new feels terrifying, what if you're not the best? This fear can keep you stuck, missing out on awesome experiences.
- Relationship Strains: If you extend your perfectionism to how others "should" behave, you might come across as con-

trolling or critical, pushing friends and family away without meaning to.

The bottom line? Uncontrolled perfectionism can sneakily hijack your happiness. It whispers, "You'll never be good enough," even though that's the least helpful thing you need to hear. You can combat perfectionism by focusing on growth.

What Perfectionism Feels Like in the Body

You're not just imagining that tense feeling in your shoulders when you're obsessing over a paper or the racing heart when you think about messing up. Perfectionism can show up physically, too:

- Tension & Tight Muscles: Constant worry about doing everything "just right" can lead to sore shoulders, neck stiffness, or headaches.
- Clenched Jaw or Teeth Grinding: Stress can set up camp in your jaw, leading to nighttime teeth grinding or random jaw aches.
- Knotted Stomach: Ever feel that twisty, anxious pit in your belly before presenting something you must nail? That's your body bracing for perceived failure.
- Fast Heartbeat & Shallow Breathing: All that pressure to perform can send your fight-or-flight response into overdrive, making your chest feel tight.
- Exhaustion: Spending mental energy on tiny details or re-checking your work a zillion times can zap your energy, leaving you drained by midday.

Recognizing these body signals is crucial. It's your system saying, "Hey, we're stressed!" The good news? The moment you ease off that perfectionist accelerator, your muscles, heart rate, and breathing can settle back down.

Ready to learn some powerful ways to *tame* your inner perfectionist? Up next, we'll explore expert advice and actionable strategies that can help you balance ambition with self-compassion, and trust me, that's a combo worth mastering!

Expert Advice

Dr. Carol Dweck found that students who adopt a growth mindset, believing their intelligence and skills can grow, are more resilient and proactive. Rather than thinking, "I'm terrible at math, so I'll fail," growth mindset thinkers say, "I can learn math if I put in the effort." The difference is subtle but *life-changing*.

Actionable Strategies

A Growth Mindset Ninja uses the **F.L.O.W.** method to embrace growth over perfection:

F – Face Your Fear: Write down exactly *what* scares you about making mistakes. Is it disappointing others? Feeling embarrassed? Identifying the fear shrinks its power.

L – Limit Unrealistic Standards: Instead of "straight A's or bust," try "I'll aim for a strong B+ or better in my toughest class." This frees you to learn without drowning in pressure.

O – Observe and Adjust: If something goes wrong, treat it like a science experiment. *"Interesting, that strategy didn't work, what's another angle?"*

W – Work in Chunks: Break tasks into bite-sized pieces, rewarding yourself for finishing each chunk. Small wins keep you energized and reduce burnout.

Now that you've got the **F.L.O.W.** framework in your toolbox, let's explore how these principles come to life in everyday teen scenarios.

Relatable Scenarios

Scenario 1: The Overworked Essay

You've revised your essay so many times you've practically memorized the dictionary. Deadline's tomorrow, and you still want to keep tweaking.
- » Growth Mindset Move: Hit "submit." Then, if needed, learn from teacher feedback afterward. Sometimes "done" is better than "perfect."

Scenario 2: The Unplayed Violin

You love music but avoid auditioning for the school orchestra because you think you're "not good enough" yet.
- » Growth Mindset Move: Try out anyway. Even if your first attempt isn't flawless, you'll learn from the experience, and probably meet new music-loving friends.

Scenario 3: Social Media Freeze

You want to post your artwork online but worry it's not "Instagram-worthy."
- » Growth Mindset Move: Post it with pride! Focus on genuine feedback over likes. You might find supportive communities that help you improve.

"**Done** is better than perfect." – Sheryl Sandberg

Personal Story

I once decided that the *perfect* birthday present for my mom would be a homemade cake, fluffy layers, fancy frosting, the works. Naturally, I found a recipe that looked like it belonged on a celebrity chef's magazine picture, and I set out to recreate it. Easy enough, right?

Well, after two hours of whisking batter (to "the precise consistency") and measuring ingredients to the milligram, I realized my oven had been preheating for so long it felt like a mini volcano. I nervously slid my masterpiece inside and watched it…sag, then rise, then transform into something resembling a lopsided volcano itself.

Undeterred, I moved on to the frosting, Italian meringue buttercream. Spoiler alert: that's code for "way too complicated for a first-time baker." By the time I finished, powdered sugar snowed across the kitchen, and the frosting was an odd shade of beige. Did I panic? Absolutely. But I slathered it on anyway, hoping taste would triumph over looks.

When I finally presented the cake, it looked like a questionable piece of modern art. *Not* the picture-perfect creation I had in mind. But you know what? My mom laughed, gave me a big hug, and declared it delicious, because it was. After all that stress, I realized the cake's imperfections made for a way better memory (and a hilarious story). Sure, it wasn't a professional bakery masterpiece, but it was 100% made with love, and that's what counted.

I realized perfectionism had robbed me of the joy in the process, until I let go and just enjoyed creating something for my mom.

Case Study: The School Play Pressure

Ava dreamed of landing the lead role in the spring musical. She practiced every line to the point where her mirror probably needed earplugs. On audition day, stage lights beamed down, and Ava

forgot an entire chunk of dialogue.
- Her Reaction: Panic. Mortification. But rather than bursting into tears (like she feared she would), she improvised a few words, did her best to stay in character, and pulled through.
- The Outcome: She didn't get the lead, but she did score a smaller (yet super-fun) supporting role. More importantly, she realized that her biggest success wasn't nailing every line, but daring to audition in the first place.

Quick Quiz Box

Which of the following helps reduce perfectionism?

- A) Doing everything alone to avoid being judged
- B) Breaking tasks into smaller steps and celebrating mini-wins
- C) Avoiding new activities unless you're guaranteed success
- D) Constantly comparing your work to everyone else's

(Answer: B – Celebrating mini-wins keeps you motivated and quells that inner critic.)

Journal Reflection Box

Write about a time you were so focused on doing something perfectly that you forgot to enjoy it. How might a growth mindset have shifted your outlook? What would you do differently now?

Action Challenge Chart

Perfectionism Trigger	Growth Mindset Action	How It Made Me Fee
Class presentation jitters	Rehearse with a friend first for feedback	More confident, less anxious
Messed up cookie recipe	Ask someone else to taste-test & tweak	Playful, less stressed
Afraid to join debate club	Attend one meeting just to observe	Curious, open to learning

By reflecting on these everyday challenges and growth-minded adjustments, we can now highlight the core lessons from Chapter 1.

Chapter 1 Key Takeaways

1. Progress > Perfection. A "good enough" draft beats endless revision.
2. Observe & Adjust. View mistakes as data for improvement.
3. Balance. High standards are great, until they overload you with stress.

Mini-FAQ

Q1: What if I keep missing my own standards anyway?
A: Use the F.L.O.W. method. Face your fear of falling short, Limit perfectionist thinking, Observe what you've done right, and Work in small steps. Your "standard" can shift as you learn.

Q2: Am I lowering my ambition by not aiming for perfect?
A: Not at all! Being a Growth Mindset Ninja means striving for excellence, not obsessing. Real growth happens when you're

courageous enough to make mistakes and learn from them.

Moving from 'perfect' to 'progress,' next we'll discover how a single word, 'yet', turns roadblocks into stepping stones.

2

EMBRACING THE POWER OF "YET"

Have you ever caught yourself thinking, *"I'm just not good at math,"* or *"I'll never learn to play the guitar"*? Those are classic fixed-mindset phrases, where you're convinced you either have a natural gift for something…or you don't. Growth Mindset Ninja begs to differ.

A growth mindset says your abilities aren't set in stone; they grow with practice, feedback, and a healthy dose of grit. When you tack on that tiny word *"yet"*, as in "I'm not good at math yet", you unlock the possibility of improvement and push aside any notion that your potential is stuck on "low."

- Fuels Persistence: Believing you *can* learn something keeps you motivated to try again, even if you're struggling.
- Fosters Curiosity: A growth mindset encourages you to explore new challenges rather than running the other way.
- Builds Resilience: Instead of labeling yourself a "failure," you see mistakes as stepping stones, each one a clue about how to get better next time.

A Growth Mindset Ninja knows it's not about blind positivity; it's about turning each roadblock into a rest stop where you gather your wits, refuel on determination, and keep cruising toward your goals.

Different Types of Mindsets

It's easy to think of mindset as either "fixed" or "growth," but there can be shades of gray:

- The All-or-Nothing Fixer
  - » Believes traits and talents are predetermined. If they're bad at something once, they're convinced they'll always be bad at it, so why bother?
- The Selective Grower
  - » Shows a growth mindset in some areas (like sports), but has a rigid "I'm hopeless" mindset in others (like math or public speaking).
- The Yet Embracer
  - » Actively uses the word "yet": "I can't do this…yet." This person hunts for strategies or tools to improve, even if the path looks rocky.
- The Undecided
  - » Flip-flops between "Maybe I can learn this if I keep trying" and "Ugh, who am I kidding?", they see glimpses of their potential but worry their efforts won't pay off.

Chances are, you've danced between these categories. Some days you might channel unstoppable optimism, while other days you're certain you'll never conquer that new dance routine. Recognizing these patterns is step one in rewiring your approach to challenges.

The Sneaky Consequences of a Fixed Mindset

A fixed mindset can steal your thunder in ways you might not see until it's too late:

- Stalled Progress: If you believe you've "already peaked" or "just aren't good" at something, you're less likely to put in the effort needed to improve.
- Fear of Failure: You might avoid tough tasks or new experiences entirely, terrified that messing up will prove you're "not smart" or "not talented."
- Low Self-Confidence: Internalizing "I can't" undermines your sense of worth, leaving you anxious or defeated before you've even begun.
- Stunted Creativity: In a fixed mindset, you'll stick to what you know. That means no experimenting, no risk-taking, and no discovering hidden abilities.
- Blaming Others or Circumstances: Sometimes, it's easier to say, "The teacher's unfair" or "That test was impossible" than to admit you need to refine your study methods.

A fixed mindset essentially hits the brakes on growth. Instead of learning from mistakes, it sees them as proof you shouldn't have tried in the first place. Not exactly the recipe for success (or happiness).

How It Applies in Real Life / How It Affects You in Life

Academics: If you bomb a quiz, you don't throw in the towel, you study differently, seek a tutor, and keep practicing until you improve.

Hobbies & Sports: You try new techniques, drills, or methods, knowing every stumble is a lesson, not an embarrassment.

Long-Term Goals: Want to learn a language, play guitar, or start a small business? The power of "yet" keeps your momentum going even when progress feels slow.

What a Growth Mindset Feels Like in the Body

Shifting to a growth mindset doesn't just alter your thoughts, it can change your *physical* response to challenges:

- Eager Anticipation
    » You might still feel nervous tackling something new (like a basketball tryout or a coding challenge), but there's a current of excitement coursing through you, too: *"Hey, maybe I can learn this!"*
- Lower Stress Levels
    » Instead of catastrophizing every slip-up, you see mistakes as normal. That perspective keeps cortisol (the stress hormone) from skyrocketing, leaving you calmer and more focused.
- A Balanced Heartbeat
    » Rather than pounding in panic, your heart might thump with determination. You're energized, but not in fight-or-flight mode.
- Steady Breathing
    » With a growth mindset, you're less likely to hyperventilate over a single misstep. Deep, measured breaths replace shallow gasps, fueling your brain with oxygen to keep problem-solving.
- Physical Confidence
    » When you feel more open to trial and error, your posture changes, shoulders back, head up. You're not bracing for defeat; you're leaning into possibility.

Recognizing these signals can help you lean deeper into your growth mindset. If you notice you're calmer and more curious than scared, that's a sign your mental gears are turning the right way.

Ready to see how a Growth Mindset Ninja takes "I can't" and adds "yet," transforming obstacles into springboards? Next, we'll dive into expert advice and actionable strategies you can use, both on days you feel unstoppable *and* on days you think your potential is tapped out. Because with a growth mindset, every stumble is just another step in the right direction.

Expert Advice

Dr. Carol Dweck, who pioneered the concept of growth mindset, found that students who embrace challenges and learn from criticism tend to outperform those who shy away from difficulty. The word "yet" is a powerful tool, it reminds you that your ability to succeed grows with each attempt.

Actionable Strategies

A Growth Mindset Ninja understands the magic of *yet*.
1. **Catch Fixed Mindset Thoughts**
   » Each time you think, "I'll never get this," tack on "yet." It's a quick way to shift from *hopeless to hopeful*.
2. **Try Something Just Beyond Your Comfort Zone**
   » If you're a beginner at piano, learn a piece that's slightly above your skill level. Embrace the challenge, and trust that repetition will get you there.
3. **Learn from Mistakes**
   » Next time you fail a test or drop the ball in a big game, ask yourself, "What can I do differently next time?" That question turns a failure into a stepping stone.
4. **Share Your Journey**
   » Talk with a friend or mentor about your progress. Hearing their perspectives and celebrating small wins together solidifies your commitment to growth.

Relatable Scenarios

Scenario 1: Language Learning Woes

You keep messing up verb conjugations in Spanish. Add "yet" to your vocabulary: "I don't remember them yet, but each practice session helps."

Scenario 2: Missed the Track Team Cut

You didn't make the final roster, this time. Now you focus on strength training, running drills, and preparing for next year's tryouts.

Scenario 3: Struggling with Public Speaking

Stage fright is real, but repeating "I'm not comfortable with speeches yet" encourages you to practice in front of friends until the butterflies calm down.

"Anyone who has never made a mistake has never tried anything new." – Albert Einstein

Personal Story

I used to believe I'd never be a decent writer, especially after a sophomore-year essay came back drenched in red ink. Seeing every suggestion and correction made me think, "Well, that's it. I'm just not good at writing." That mindset stuck with me until I heard someone talk about the "power of yet." Instead of saying "I'm not good at this," you say "I'm not good at this yet," leaving room to grow.

I started whispering, "I'm not a great writer yet," whenever self-doubt creeped in. It wasn't magic, but it was enough to change how I approached homework. Instead of dreading feedback, I hunted for tips to improve, reading articles, watching videos, and asking friends how they planned their essays. That little shift in perspective nudged me forward, and soon my English teacher noticed the difference. An email arrived: "You've improved. Consider applying for Honors English next year?"

My first reaction? Total disbelief. Honors was for "real" writers. But that yet mantra pushed me to try. Even though those tougher assignments felt intimidating, I kept telling myself that every misstep was just part of the learning curve. By junior year, I was actually enjoying the process, finding new ways to structure arguments and craft introductions. The "red ink" turned into focused feedback I could use to get better.

One day, I turned in a research paper and got an A-. My teacher wrote, "Keep experimenting, your voice is coming through!" That's when I realized I wasn't doomed to mediocrity. Each challenge just pointed me toward the next step. By the end of the year, I even volunteered to share my essays in class, something I'd never have done before. The biggest lesson? Adding "yet" to my doubts gave me room to improve. Now, whenever something seems daunting, I remind myself that I'm not there...*yet*.

Quick Quiz Box

Which phrase demonstrates a growth mindset?

- • A) "I'll never understand algebra!"
- • B) "I'm not good at algebra yet."
- • C) "I failed a quiz, so there's no point trying."
- • D) "Math is impossible."

(Answer: B. That one little word, "yet," signals you believe in your ability to improve.)

Journal Reflection Box

Think of a skill or subject you struggle with. Write a few sentences using "yet." For example: "I can't shoot three-pointers yet, but I'm working on my form."

Action Challenge Chart

Goal / Challenge	Add "Yet" Phrase	Small Step Forward
Improving my writing	"I'm not a great writer yet…"	Write a short story daily
Understanding chemistry	"I don't get chemical equations yet"	Review one concept at a time
Building confidence on stage	"I'm not comfortable speaking in public yet"	Practice a speech for a friend

A Growth Mindset Ninja realizes that potential isn't fixed, it evolves with every effort. By harnessing the power of "yet," you can transform frustration into focus, doubt into determination, and challenges into victories. The journey is yours, keep moving forward, one "yet" at a time!

Chapter 2 Key Takeaways

1. "Yet" = Possibility. Adding that tiny word transforms "I can't" into "I'm learning."
2. Failure as Feedback. Each stumble teaches you how to adjust.
3. Keep Experimenting. Growth is a skill you build over time, not a fixed trait.

Mini-FAQ

Q1: What if I keep failing and I can't see any improvement?
A: Reflect on your approach, are you practicing effectively, or repeating mistakes without adjusting? Sometimes you need fresh

methods (tutor, study group, coaching). "Yet" reminds you you're still in progress.

Q2: How do I handle friends who say 'you're just not good at that'? A: Invite them to watch you practice or show them small improvements. A growth mindset is contagious, if they see you leveling up, they might rethink their doubt.

With 'yet' fueling your growth, it's time to learn how to laugh off awkward moments and rise from embarrassment even stronger.

3

LAUGHING OFF AWKWARDNESS

You walk into homeroom feeling like you've got your life together, then bam! you trip over your own shoelace right in front of your entire class. Your cheeks light up like neon signs, your heart races, and all you can think is, *"Everyone saw that! I'm never living this down!"*

Whether it's mixing up someone's name, forgetting your lines in a school play, or accidentally texting the wrong person, embarrassment happens. But here's the thing: a little blush doesn't have to ruin your day, or your confidence. Embarrassment matters because it highlights what we value (like our image or other people's opinions), and when we learn to cope with it, we reclaim our freedom to be ourselves, stumbles, bloopers, and all.

- It's a Shared Human Experience: Everyone has that cringe story. Realizing you're not alone can ease your self-consciousness.
- It Can Paralyze or Propel You: Handled poorly, embarrassment can keep you from ever speaking up again. Handled well, it can give you the resilience to laugh, learn, and carry on.

Growth Mindset swoops in to remind us that a trip, a slip, or a word-fumble isn't the end, it might even be the start of a great story.

Different Types of Embarrassment

Not all embarrassing moments are created equal. You might recognize yourself in one or more of these categories:

1. The Clumsy Commotion
   » You're prone to physical mishaps, spilling drinks, walking into doors, dropping your lunch tray. It's like the universe said, *"We need someone to demonstrate gravity daily."*
2. The Social Slip-Up
   » You accidentally call your teacher "Dad," forget someone's name mid-conversation, or laugh way too loudly at a joke that wasn't funny. Awkward stares ensue.
3. The Personal Blooper
   » Your outfit rips, you get a huge stain on your pants, or you realize halfway through the day your shirt's on backward. These moments make you want to hide under a desk… forever.
4. The Digital Disaster
   » You send a text to the wrong group chat, post something you instantly regret, or realize your mic was never muted in an online class. Technology can magnify the cringe factor!

Each scenario might leave you feeling mortified, but the good news is that everyone experiences these from time to time. Recognizing your typical "brand" of embarrassment can help you prepare, and recover, more easily.

The Sneaky Consequences of Uncontrolled Embarrassment

When embarrassment hijacks your confidence, it can have ripple effects you might not even realize:

- Social Withdrawal: If you're constantly worried about doing something "embarrassing," you might avoid social events, missing out on friendships and experiences.
- Overthinking & Anxiety: Instead of remembering the hundred things you did right today, you replay that *one awkward* moment in your head on loop, blowing it out of proportion.
- Self-Censorship: You stop contributing ideas in group projects or volunteering to read aloud in class because you fear messing up. In reality, speaking up is how you get better.
- People-Pleasing: Sometimes, to dodge embarrassment, you overly try to fit in, abandoning your own preferences or style just to avoid standing out.
- Impact on Mood: Constantly anticipating cringe-worthy moments can sour your mood, making you more irritable, self-critical, or impatient with others.

Embarrassment might seem like a small, fleeting emotion, but when left unchecked, it can shape how you see yourself and how you engage with the world. But guess what? Embarrassed Ninja is here to help you identify it and manage it better.

What Embarrassment Feels Like in the Body

It's not just a mental thing, your body reacts like you're in real danger:

- Flushed Face & Ears: Your body diverts blood to your face, turning you into a human tomato. It's basically a big neon sign that says, "I FEEL AWKWARD!"
- Racing Heartbeat: Your heart pounds as if you're about to wrestle a bear, even though you've just tripped on a pencil.
- Butterflies (or Pterodactyls) in Your Stomach: That lurch in your gut arrives because your fight-or-flight system kicks into gear, your body can't tell if it's social embarrassment or a hungry tiger.
- Sweaty Palms & Armpits: Nothing says "I'm panicking" like damp hands or suspicious pit stains. Your body's trying to cool you down, even though it's only your feelings that are on fire.

- Short, Shallow Breaths: You may catch yourself sucking in air like you've just sprinted a mile, even if you're standing perfectly still.

These physical sensations, although uncomfortable, are your body's alarm bells telling you, "We care about social approval, and we're in *warning* mode!" Once you realize it's a normal response, you can see past the panic and remind yourself that embarrassment is rarely fatal (even if it feels that way in the moment).

Ready to learn how a Growth Mindset Ninja bounces back from a faceplant, or an oops moment in front of an audience? Up next, we'll check out expert advice and actionable strategies to help you transform your cringe-worthy slip-ups into growth opportunities (and maybe even a good laugh). Because if you can't find the humor in your own bloopers, you're missing out on half the fun of being human!

Actionable Strategies

Now that you know how embarrassment can tie your stomach in knots (and turn your face the color of a cherry lollipop), it's time to learn how to bounce back like a pro. Introducing **S.H.I.N.E.**, a set of simple, yet powerful, steps that help you keep your cool, and maybe even share a laugh, whenever you take a clumsy tumble or say the wrong thing. Because, let's face it: life's way too short to stay stuck in cringe mode. Let's move forward, together!

S: Stop and Breathe: Pause for a quick, deep breath. This mini "time-out" can lower your heart rate and clear your head.

H: Humor: Find the comedy in your situation, even if it's a small chuckle about how clumsy you feel. Laughter breaks the tension.

I: Identify the Lesson: Ask yourself, "What can I learn here?" Maybe you'll walk more carefully, double-check your spelling, or prep more thoroughly next time.

N: Normalize: Everyone makes mistakes. Everyone. Reassure yourself this isn't a once-in-a-century goof, just another human slip.

E: Embrace the Moment: Own the situation, show resilience, and move forward with confidence. Sometimes your biggest embarrassment becomes a hilarious story down the road.

With **S.H.I.N.E.**, you turn cringe-worthy into character-building and relatable to others.

Relatable Scenarios

Scenario 1: Wrong Name in Public

You wave enthusiastically at someone who looks like your friend, only to realize you've never met them before. S.H.I.N.E. by cracking a small joke: "You look just like my best friend. Surprise cameo!"

Scenario 2: Presentation Gone Awry

Your slideshow won't load, and you freeze. Take a breath, make a silly comment like, "Guess my slides wanted a day off," and speak from memory, people often admire quick thinking more than flawless tech.

Scenario 3: Text Mishap

You accidentally text the wrong person. S.H.I.N.E. by apologizing, then adding a lighthearted twist. "Oops, guess it's time for me to label my contacts properly!"

"**Experience** is simply the name we give our mistakes." – Oscar Wilde

Personal Story

I still remember the day I dashed out the door, already late, and hustled into school, juggling a backpack, a messy stack of papers, and the remnants of my half-eaten breakfast. I was feeling rushed but confident enough, I'd managed to finish my history essay the night before, and I was mentally preparing for a big group presentation that morning. I didn't realize, however, that I'd missed one crucial detail: my jeans zipper was completely undone.

By the time I got to first period, I'd already passed a dozen people in the hallway, teachers, friends, a couple of older students whose names I didn't even know. I greeted them, gave them nods and half-smiles, and kept barreling forward, blissfully unaware of my unzipped predicament. It wasn't until I plopped into my desk and caught my friend's wide-eyed stare that I noticed something was off.

"Um," she whispered, eyes darting toward my waist. "I don't know how to tell you this, but your, uh…zipper."

My face went from rosy to scorching in record time. Suddenly, I remembered how I'd yanked my jeans on in a hurry, skipping both breakfast clean-up and, apparently, the final step of zipping up. My mind raced, replaying every interaction I'd had that morning. I pictured teachers who might have glanced down at my undone zipper, the older students who might have snickered behind me, the friend who probably noticed but was too polite to say anything. In that moment, I wanted to bury myself in my oversized hoodie and vanish.

But here's the twist: the rest of the day, once I zipped up, of course, turned out to be surprisingly…okay. Sure, my cheeks stayed flushed for a good hour, but something unexpected happened whenever I mustered the courage to laugh at myself. When I quietly admitted to people, "Oh my goodness, I walked around all morning with my zipper down," they didn't make fun of me or roll their eyes. Most burst into sympathetic giggles. A couple even told me their own horror stories, like the time they wore their shirt inside out for half a day or accidentally tucked their skirt into their tights.

It was like my embarrassing moment turned into a conversation starter. Instead of a humiliating memory, it became a shared experience that reminded me everyone does cringe-worthy things sometimes. By lunch, my blunder wasn't a source of shame, more like a silly anecdote. A friend teased me gently by handing me a neon-colored sticky note that said, "ZIP CHECK!" which made us both laugh so hard we nearly spilled our drinks.

Looking back, that morning taught me a big lesson about vulnerability and empathy. Embarrassing moments can feel like the end of the world, like a spotlight you never asked for, highlighting every bit of your awkwardness. But if you own the moment, zip up (literally or figuratively), and allow people to laugh with you rather than cringe at you, it can transform an "oops" into a bonding moment. Turns out, a busted zipper can be more than a fashion fail, it can also be a reminder that we're all human, and sometimes the most mortifying slip-ups lead to the most unexpectedly heartwarming connections.

Case Study: The School Hallway Slip

Alyssa was rushing to class, arms full of books, when she slipped on a stray pencil. Everything clattered, and a few classmates giggled. She felt her cheeks flare, but remembered S.H.I.N.E.:

- She took a deep breath (Stop).
- Cracked a quick joke: "Looks like I just invented the new hallway dance move!" (Humor).
- She realized she was rushing too much, maybe leaving earlier next time would help (Identify the Lesson).
- Reminded herself that plenty of people trip or drop stuff (Normalize).
- Picked up her books with a grin and hurried on (Embrace the Moment).

By lunch, she was laughing about it with her friends.

Quick Quiz Box

When you feel embarrassed, which is the best S.H.I.N.E. step to start with?

- A) Point out someone else's mistake
- B) Hide and never speak again
- C) Take a slow, deep breath
- D) Pretend it never happened

(Answer: C. Stopping to breathe helps reset your emotions before moving on.)

Journal Reflection Box

Write about a time you felt deeply embarrassed. Which S.H.I.N.E. step could have helped most, and how might you handle a similar situation now?

Action Challenge Chart

Embarrassing Situation	S.H.I.N.E. Step Used	Result / Feeling
Spilled juice in cafeteria	Stop, take a deep breath, then crack a small joke	Less tense, people jumped in to help
Called teacher "Mom" by accident	Embrace it with humor	Class giggled, tension eased
Forgot lines in a play	Normalize by remembering mistakes happen to everyone	Confidence to improvise

Remember: Managing embarrassment isn't about never feeling awkward, it's about rising from those moments with a grin on your face and a story worth telling. Embrace life's slip-ups, they're proof you're courageously putting yourself out there!

Chapter 3 Key Takeaways

1. Embarrassment Happens. You're not alone, everyone slips up sometimes.
2. **S.H.I.N.E.** Stop & breathe, use Humor, Identify the lesson, Normalize, Embrace it.
3. Blunders as Bonding. Sharing an "oops" moment can bring empathy and even laughter.

Mini-FAQ

Q1: What if my embarrassment is really big, like public humiliation?
A: Even big stumbles can follow S.H.I.N.E. Address it with a short apology or laugh if appropriate, remind yourself it's a universal experience, then embrace it and move on. It won't define you

forever.

Q2: People keep bringing up my embarrassing moment, how do I cope?
A: Turn it into a lighthearted anecdote before they can. By owning the story, you take away its sting. A quick "Yeah, wasn't that epic?" can diffuse ongoing teasing.

Once you embrace slip-ups, discover how bending your mindset like a ninja can help you adapt when plans go haywire.

4

BENDING THE RULES (IN A GOOD WAY)

Imagine you've carefully planned every minute of your afternoon, homework from 3:00 to 4:00, snack time at 4:05, gaming from 4:30 to 5:00, only to have your best friend text you last minute, "Can we meet up earlier?" If your first instinct is to freeze or grumble because your schedule is now ruined, you might be missing out on the magic of Flexible Thinking.

The world rarely bows to our neatly laid plans. Buses run late, group members drop out of projects, and sometimes the restaurant you've been dying to try is closed for renovations. Being flexible means you can pivot gracefully when life decides to throw you a curveball, reducing stress and unlocking creative solutions you never knew existed.

- Better Problem-Solving: Instead of panicking, you say, "Alright, what else can we do?"
- Less Anxiety: Changes don't feel like catastrophes, just minor detours.
- Stronger Friendships: People appreciate when you can adapt and compromise, especially in group work or social plans.

A Growth Mindset Ninja sees every unexpected twist as an opportunity rather than a crisis. After all, sometimes the Plan B you never wanted turns out to be the most memorable adventure of all.

Different Flavors of Rigid Thinking

Before diving into flexibility, let's meet the culprits that hold you back:

1. The Planner to the Extreme
   » You love your schedules and to-do lists a lot. When something disrupts your carefully crafted plan, you feel like the sky is falling.
2. The 'Only One Right Way' Thinker
   » You believe there's exactly one correct method for doing a task (like studying or cleaning), and any deviation is "wrong." This can cause tension with people who do things differently.
3. The Perfectionist Partner
   » If you're also a perfectionist, you might resist trying new approaches for fear they won't be good enough. You'd rather do it the "old way" than risk failing at a new method.
4. The Comfort-Zone Camper
   » Sticking to routine feels safe. Venturing outside can feel uncomfortable, so you shy away from anything unfamiliar, even if it's potentially awesome.

Recognize one or more of these patterns? Don't worry; that just means you have a perfect spot to start leveling up your flexibility game.

The Sneaky Consequences of Rigid Thinking

When you refuse to adapt, you may not realize the chain reaction it causes:

- Sky-High Stress: If any change sends you into a tailspin, life becomes exhausting, because, let's face it, change is always lurking.
- Missed Opportunities: You might ignore new ideas or experiences just because they weren't in your original plan. Who knows what epic memories you're skipping?
- Tense Relationships: Being unwilling to compromise can strain friendships. Nobody likes feeling pressured to follow a single script, your way, or the highway.
- Delayed Problem-Solving: Instead of finding a quick workaround, you might waste time lamenting that your Plan A crashed.

Clinging too hard to "the way things must be" can make every speed bump feel like a road closure, and that's a surefire route to frustration and burnout. But fear not, Flexible Thinking Ninja has your back.

What Rigid Thinking Feels Like in the Body

Just like any emotional state, inflexibility can show up physically:

- Tight Shoulders & Neck: Rigid thinking often pairs with literal rigidity in your posture. Your muscles tense up as if bracing for a fight.
- Upset Stomach: Anxiety about things "not going right" can lead to that telltale queasy feeling or butterflies that won't calm down.
- Increased Heart Rate: Stress hormones kick in when reality doesn't match your expectations, your body goes on alert, thinking it needs to "fight" the situation.
- Clenched Jaw or Grinding Teeth: When you refuse to bend, the tension can show up in your jaw. You might notice soreness or headaches.
- Mental Exhaustion: Constantly resisting change drains mental energy. Think of it like swimming against a current; you're using a ton of effort just to stay in one spot.

Recognizing these signs is your body's way of saying, "Hey, lighten up! We can pivot if we need to."

Ready to discover how a Growth Mindset Ninja navigates everyday curveballs? Next, we'll jump into expert advice and actionable strategies, so you can keep your cool (and maybe even find a few pleasant surprises) when life veers off-script.

Expert Advice

Dr. Adam Grant, an organizational psychologist, often talks about the power of "rethinking", challenging your assumptions to find new solutions. He suggests that being curious and open-minded is key to discovering better approaches. By welcoming the unknown, you become more resilient and innovative, even if your first idea doesn't pan out.

Actionable Strategies

A Growth Mindset relies on the **Three Ts** to keep the mind agile:

Try Making New Rules for Games
 » The next time you're playing a board game or even a video game, bend the rules (with everyone's agreement, of course). Try a "no talking" challenge in a group game, or come up with a "wild card" that changes the objective. This trains your brain to look for variations and realize there's rarely just one right way to play, or live.

Tell Jokes That Play with Meanings and Sounds of Words
 » Get punny! Language is flexible, and so are you. Think of words with multiple meanings or homophones (like "flower" and "flour"), and try to craft silly, pun-based jokes. Playing with words is like mental gymnastics, boosting your creativity and your sense of humor.

Think Out Loud About All Possible Solutions to a Problem
 » When faced with a dilemma, like how to spend your weekend or tackle a difficult homework assignment, talk through every

option, even the silly ones. Saying them out loud can spark unexpected ideas. Brainstorm first, then narrow down. You might be surprised by the gems hidden in your "bad" ideas.

Now that we've explored the Three Ts for building mental flexibility, let's see how they play out in everyday teen scenarios that call for agile thinking.

Relatable Scenarios

Scenario 1: The Class Presentation Switcheroo

You planned to show slides, but the projector is broken. Instead of panicking, you create a quick poster on the fly. Bonus points if you find items around the room (like colored markers, sticky notes) and turn your talk into an interactive game.

Scenario 2: Spontaneous Party Themes

You and your friends have a movie night planned, but the power goes out. You gather flashlights and turn the night into a campfire story session. Adapting the plan keeps the fun alive.

Scenario 3: Group Project Clash

Two friends want a serious topic for your social studies project, while another wants something humorous. You compromise by weaving humor into serious facts, maybe a "superhero newscast" about historical events. Everyone's perspective is honored, and the project stands out.

"The measure of intelligence is the ability to change."
– Albert Einstein

Personal Story

When I was in sixth grade, I was absolutely convinced that the best way to get top marks on my science fair project was to memorize every fact about *volcanic rocks*. My booth looked polished, and I had bullet points for days, until the judge asked me a question about how volcanoes affect local wildlife. I hadn't studied that at all.

Cue the blank stare.

In that heart-stopping moment, my best friend (who'd done her project on amphibians) blurted out a random fact about frogs inhabiting volcanic lakes. The judge raised an eyebrow, I awkwardly tried to connect the dots, and soon we were half-improvising, half-flailing. To my surprise, the judge grinned. She was excited that we were *thinking on our feet*, not just rattling off rote memorization. Even though we didn't have the "perfect" answer, we rolled with it, cracking jokes about "lava-lovin' frogs" (which don't exist, sadly).

We didn't win first place, but we got compliments for our creativity. I learned that being open-minded, even silly at times, can turn a near-disaster into a memorable moment. Now, I research every angle of a topic, but I also give myself permission to pivot when someone throws me an unexpected question. Because real life? It's full of curveballs, and flexible thinking is your best catcher's mitt. Our unplanned pivot, our 'Try something new' approach, proved that flexible thinking can be your best asset when your plan collapses.

Case Study: The Multi-Club Conundrum

Brandon wanted to join the debate club, but it clashed with soccer practice on Tuesdays. At first, he was bummed and considered quitting the club altogether. Then, he flexed his thinking:
- He talked to his coach about practicing with the team three days a week and training on his own on Tuesdays.
- He asked the debate coach if he could attend recorded

practice sessions online to stay caught up.

Both agreed, and Brandon ended up juggling both passions. His flexible approach not only solved the schedule issue but also impressed coaches who loved his go-getter attitude.

Quick Quiz Box

Which approach best demonstrates flexible thinking when your phone dies?

- A) Sulk because you can't message your friends.
- B) Blame the phone company for not inventing an indestructible battery.
- C) Ask a friend for a charger and read a book while you wait.
- D) Tape your phone to a potato in a bizarre science experiment.

(Answer: C. Resourceful and calm, bonus points if you actually try D just for the laughs, though!)

Journal Reflection Box

Think back to a time you were stuck in a situation that didn't go your way. How did you react? Brainstorm at least two other ways you could have responded. Which one seems the most creative or fun?

Action Challenge Chart

Situation	Flexible Thinking Move	Outcome/Feeling
Unexpected quiz in class	Ask if you can use scratch paper to organize thoughts	Less panic, more clarity
Friend cancels movie plans	Suggest a virtual watch party instead	Still fun, plus minimal travel!
Car ride gets delayed	Create a car karaoke or word association game	Time flies, stress fades

Track your own flexible thinking experiences and see how your mind starts bending toward new possibilities instead of breaking under pressure.

Chapter 4 Key Takeaways

1. Pivot, Don't Panic. Life rarely follows your perfect plan.
2. The Three Ts. Try new rules, Tell jokes (play with words), Think through all solutions.
3. Small Shifts. Adjusting your approach can unlock creative, less stressful outcomes.

Mini-FAQ

Q1: What if I genuinely can't find a Plan B?
A: Start by brainstorming every idea, especially the silly or half-baked ones. Telling jokes or rewriting "rules" can inspire new angles. Sometimes a wild idea leads to an actual solution.

Q2: How do I handle peer pressure if friends don't like my 'flexible' approach?

A: Remind them there's rarely one "right way." Offer to compromise or try a blend of your ideas. Flexibility is about everyone benefiting from a new angle, not just you.

Shifting gracefully under change is one skill, but now let's confront fear head-on, step by shaky step.

5

FACING FEAR WITH COURAGE (EVEN IF YOUR KNEES ARE SHAKING)

Have you ever felt your heart pound so hard you thought it would bust out of your chest? Maybe it was right before giving a class presentation, stepping onto a stage, or even just walking into a new club meeting for the first time. That burst of terror, the sweaty palms, the sudden urge to flee the scene? That's fear making its grand entrance.

Fear isn't all bad, it keeps us from petting wild tigers and crossing the street without looking both ways. But when fear starts yelling "DANGER!" at every little challenge, whether it's talking to someone new, trying a tough subject in school, or auditioning for the school musical, that's when it becomes a roadblock. A Growth Mindset Ninja steps in to remind us that courage isn't about *never* being afraid, it's about feeling the fear and doing what you need to do anyway.

- Healthy Alarm System: Fear can protect you from real threats.
- Opportunity Thief: Taken too far, it steals your chances to explore, grow, and experience life's adventures.

Life's brimming with possibilities, but fear can tie you to a boring corner where everything feels "safe" (and often, unexciting). This ninja knows you don't have to be fearless to be brave, you just need the right tools to keep fear in check.

Different Faces of Fear

Fear can show up wearing a variety of disguises:

1. The Classic Stage Fright
   » Your knees quake, your voice shakes, and your mind blanks when attention is on you. One forgotten line and you'd rather dig a hole to hide in.
2. The "What-If" Overthinker
   » You imagine every possible worst-case scenario, if you try out for soccer, you'll trip, fall, break your ankle, and let your team down, all in the first five minutes.
3. The 'No Way, Not Today' Avoider
   » When fear surfaces, you bolt. You'd rather miss a promising opportunity than deal with those fluttery nerves.
4. The Sudden Panic Button
   » Sometimes fear hits out of nowhere, like a pop quiz you didn't see coming, and you freeze up, mentally screaming, "I can't do this!"

Each type of fear can shut doors that were never truly locked. Recognizing what flavor of fear you wrestle with can help you figure out how to tame it.

The Sneaky Consequences of Uncontrolled Fear

When fear goes from being your inner guard dog to a giant troll blocking your path, it silently chips away at your day-to-day life:

- Missed Opportunities: Saying "no" to that debate team or study-abroad trip just because you might fail or feel awkward.

- Lower Self-Confidence: The more you avoid what scares you, the more you start believing you can't handle tough stuff.
- Isolation: You might back out of social events or group outings, afraid you'll do or say something embarrassing.
- Increased Anxiety: Fear can metastasize into a constant "what if" loop in your head, making everyday decisions feel monumental.
- Regret: Looking back and realizing you let fear run the show instead of giving something a chance.

Fear's sneakiest trick is convincing you it's saving you from disaster, when in reality, it's often robbing you of experiences that could help you grow.

How It Applies in Real Life / How It Affects You in Life

- Friendships & Dating: Fear of rejection can stop you from saying hi or sharing your real feelings.
- Academics & Activities: Fear of failure might keep you from exploring a new club or tackling a challenging subject.
- Future Goals: Dream big! Fear can whisper, "What if I'm not good enough?" But ignoring that whisper lets you chase your ambitions.

What Fear Feels Like in the Body

Remember those sweaty palms and the heart doing the cha-cha? Physically, fear can put on quite the performance:

- Racing Heart & Quick Breaths: Your body floods with adrenaline, gearing up for "fight or flight."
- Shaky Limbs: Your muscles tense, preparing to either sprint away or defend yourself.
- Butterflies (or Pterodactyls) in Your Stomach: Digestion grinds to a halt, resulting in that signature swirl of nausea or jitters.

- Tunnel Vision: You might become hyper-focused on the "threat," forgetting there's a bigger picture beyond it.
- Excessive Sweating: Your body's attempt to cool off, thinking you're about to exert yourself in some epic showdown.

These sensations aren't just random betrayals, they're your system's age-old survival response. The good news is that many fears we face today aren't life-or-death, so we can learn to soothe those overblown alarms.

Ready to see how a Growth Mindset Ninja transforms knee-knocking moments into stepping stones toward bravery? Next, we'll dive into expert advice and actionable strategies that'll help you face fear, even if your voice shakes, your palms sweat, and your heart tries to tap-dance out of your chest. After all, courage doesn't mean never being afraid, it means taking that shaky step forward anyway.

Expert Advice

Many therapists recommend exposure therapy: facing your fears in tiny, manageable doses. By repeatedly doing the thing that scares you (in a safe way), your brain learns it's not so dangerous after all. The L.I.O.N. method is a simplified version of that idea, guiding you to approach fear step by step.

Actionable Strategies

A Growth Mindset Ninja knows the **L.I.O.N.** hack can help overcome fear.

L – Look Around: Take a moment to see where you are and notice that you're safe.
- » If you're in math class, chances are no actual lions are roaming the halls (except this metaphorical one!). Ground yourself by scanning the room and realizing nothing is truly threatening.

I – Imagine a Happy Place: Think of a place that makes you feel cozy and carefree, maybe your grandma's kitchen or a beach at sunset.
- » Visualize the sounds, smells, and sights. Ah, can you smell the cookies baking or feel the sand under your toes? This mental vacation helps keep panic at bay.

O – Open Up: Talk to someone you trust about what's scaring you.
- » Sharing your fears with a friend, parent, or counselor often makes them feel smaller and more manageable. Another bonus? They might have tips for tackling them.

N – Now Be Brave: Take a small step to face your fear, knowing you can do it.
- » Don't leap into the deep end right away, start with baby steps. If you're scared of speaking in front of crowds, try reading a poem aloud to a trusted friend first. Then build from there.

Now that you've discovered how the **L.I.O.N.** method tames your fears, let's see how it applies in everyday teen moments when facing uncertainty head-on.

Relatable Scenarios

Scenario 1: Asking for Help

Worried about looking "uncool" if you admit you're struggling with homework? Look around (safe place), imagine your favorite music fest (happy place), open up to a teacher (or friend), and take that step to ask questions.

Scenario 2: School Talent Show

Fear can make you want to skip the audition. But remember you're physically safe on stage, no meteors are crashing down. Picture yourself at home practicing (happy place). Share your nerves with a friend (open up). Finally, walk on stage (be brave) and show your stuff.

Scenario 3: Trying a Sport

Fear of embarrassing yourself might keep you on the sidelines. Check out the field or gym (look around). Picture your dream scenario of scoring the winning point (imagine). Chat with a teammate about your nerves (open up). Then jump into drills (be brave).

"**Do** one thing every day that scares you."
– Eleanor Roosevelt

Personal Story: My First Savings Goal

On a whim, I signed up to run for 6th-grade Vice President. My "campaign" was just homemade posters ("Vote Mary Nguyen: A Nguyen-er!") and lollipops handed out during homeroom. But then came the real challenge: giving a speech in front of the entire 6th grade. My stomach lurched at the thought.

That's when I used the "L.I.O.N." method:

- **Look Around**: Realize the audience is just kids like me, not a horde of critics.
- **Imagine a Happy Place**: Picture somewhere comfortable, like my living room, where messing up isn't a big deal.
- **Open Up**: Confess my nerves to a friend, who was equally terrified. Sharing the panic somehow made it easier.
- **Now Be Brave**: Step up to the mic and speak, shaky voice and all. I even squeezed in a joke about free pizza, which earned me a tiny burst of applause.

A few days later, I found out I'd won, by two votes. The real victory, though, was learning that facing my fears head-on (with sweaty palms, no less) can open doors. My voice was quivery, but it still reached the crowd. And I learned that sometimes a little courage, a bit of honesty, and, yes, a promise of pizza can go a long way.

Case Study: The Overnight Camping Trip

Jordan's class planned an overnight camping trip. He worried about wild animals, spooky stories around the campfire, and just sleeping outside in general. Using L.I.O.N.:

- Look Around: He reminded himself they had adult chaperones, tents, and supplies. No one was actually lost in the wilderness.
- Imagine a Happy Place: He pictured playing video games in

his cozy bedroom, letting the calming vibe settle his nerves.
- Open Up: He told his best friend he felt uneasy, who agreed to be tent-mates and keep a flashlight handy.
- Now Be Brave: He went on the trip, nervous but determined. In the end, he loved stargazing and realized the real "wild" was his own imagination.

Quick Quiz Box

Which part of the L.I.O.N. method involves talking to someone you trust?

- A) Look Around
- B) Imagine a Happy Place
- C) Open Up
- D) Now Be Brave

(Answer: C. "Open Up" is all about sharing your fears.)

Journal Reflection Box

Write about a fear that's been holding you back. How can you use L.I.O.N. to tackle it in small steps?

Action Challenge Chart

Fearful Moment	L.I.O.N. Step Used	Result / Feeling
Seeing a huge spider	Look Around (check it's harmless)	Realized it won't chase me, relaxed
Spooky stories at camp	Imagine a Happy Place (safe bed)	Calmed nerves, fell asleep faster
Public speaking assignment	Open Up (tell teacher/friend)	Got reassurance & practice tips

Courage beats fear, but stamina keeps you going, meet grit as your next key to unstoppable perseverance.

Chapter 5 Key Takeaways

1. Fear's Protective Side. It can keep you safe, but can also hold you back.
2. L.I.O.N.. Look around (ground yourself), Imagine comfort, Open up to someone, Now be brave with small steps.
3. Courage isn't Fearless. It's acting despite the shaking knees.

Mini-FAQ

Q1: How do I handle fear that appears out of nowhere (panic button)?
A: Go through L.I.O.N. quickly: remind yourself you're physically safe, visualize a happy spot, tell someone you trust how you feel, then take one small brave action.

Q2: Isn't it better to avoid scary stuff altogether?
A: Avoidance might feel good short-term, but it often fuels bigger anxiety long-term. Facing fear in tiny doses builds real confidence

and often leads to awesome experiences you'd miss otherwise.

You've stared down fear, now learn to flow like water when life flips your plans. Grit is next!

6

POWERING THROUGH WITH PERSEVERANCE

Ever start a big project feeling supercharged, only to get bored, stuck, or overwhelmed halfway through? Or maybe you've tried to learn a new skill (like skateboarding or guitar) and quit at the first sign of frustration. That's where grit comes in: it's the drive that says, "I'm in this for the long haul, bumps and all."

Grit matters because it's the secret sauce behind every major success story, whether you're an aspiring athlete, a future entrepreneur, or simply hoping to level up your own personal best. A Growth Mindset Ninja reminds us that talent can only take you so far, but perseverance, the ability to keep going when the going gets tough, can push you across the finish line and beyond.

- Turns Failure into Feedback: Grit helps you see mistakes as data, not dead ends.
- Builds Resilience: Life is full of curveballs. Grit is your glove for catching them without falling apart.
- Fuels Confidence: Each time you persist through a challenge, you prove to yourself you can handle even bigger hurdles next time.

Different Types of Grit

Grit doesn't have just one face. You might spot yourself in one (or more) of these categories:

1. The Goal-Getter
   » You set your eyes on a prize, like earning a black belt, finishing a marathon, or topping your class rank, and you chase it relentlessly, come rain or shine.
2. The Steady Eddy
   » You might not be the loudest or flashiest, but you're consistent. You show up day after day, inching toward improvement with calm determination.
3. The Comeback Kid
   » Failures don't keep you down for long. You stumble, dust yourself off, and rejoin the fray, often surprising people with your bounce-back ability.
4. The Slow-and-Sure
   » You're patient, methodical, and refuse to throw in the towel, even if it takes you a bit longer to grasp a concept or master a skill.

No matter your style, grit is about keeping your focus on the long game rather than short-lived glory. It's less about immediate triumphs and more about building lasting strength.

The Sneaky Consequences of Not Building Grit

When you lack perseverance, it can quietly sabotage your growth in ways you might not expect:

- Chronic Quitting: You might abandon hobbies or projects as soon as they lose their sparkle, never discovering where they might have led.
- Missed Opportunities: If you bail at the first sign of difficulty, you'll likely never find out what you could have accomplished if you'd pushed a little further.

- Low Self-Confidence: Quitting repeatedly can create a feedback loop of *"I can't do anything well,"* even though it's the lack of persistence, not ability, that's holding you back.
- Dependence on Instant Results: Without grit, you might become addicted to quick wins and give up on anything that isn't immediately rewarding.
- Fear of Long-Term Goals: Big dreams can seem scary if you're used to hitting the eject button whenever things get tough.

It's not that you have to endure every painful situation forever. But building grit means discerning which challenges are worth your time, and then sticking around to see them through.

What Grit Does to Your Brain and Body

When you stick with challenging tasks, you build mental "muscles" for resilience. Each time you refuse to quit, you reinforce neural pathways that say, *I can handle this.* Grit also helps you manage stress, because you learn to see obstacles as temporary, solvable bumps on the path, not permanent roadblocks.

How It Applies in Real Life / How It Affects You in Life

- Academics: Tough subjects or exams become less intimidating when you trust your ability to keep improving.
- Sports & Hobbies: Grit helps you endure the grueling practices that transform you from beginner to skilled player (or performer).
- Long-Term Goals: Whether it's college, a dream career, or a personal project, grit helps you stay focused when motivation dips.

What Grit Feels Like in the Body

Believe it or not, grit can change how you respond physically to stress:

- Sustained Energy: While others might get mentally drained midway, gritty folks find a second (or third) wind. Their commitment pumps out motivation that keeps fatigue at bay, at least for a while!
- Steady Heart Rate: If you're determined to keep going, your body often adapts. You might still feel pressure, but it's more of a stable hum than a wild panic.
- Deep Breathing: When you're in the groove, you learn to breathe through the hard parts, whether it's an extra lap on the track or finishing a tough homework set.
- Focused Mindset: Grit harnesses adrenaline for progress instead of letting it spiral into anxiety. You feel *locked in* rather than frantic.
- Post-Challenge Relaxation: After pushing through a rough patch, growth mindset ninjas enjoy a sense of relief and accomplishment that can feel like an internal high-five to your whole body.

Recognizing these subtle shifts can help you lean into grit even more. When you feel that surge of determination, pay attention to how your body and mind lock into place, ready to handle what comes next.

Fired up to learn how a Growth Mindset Ninja keeps going when the going gets tough? Next, we'll explore some expert advice and actionable strategies that can help you build resilience, turning short bursts of effort into long-term achievements worth celebrating. Because with grit on your side, no hurdle is too high.

Expert Advice

Psychologist Angela Duckworth, who popularized the concept of grit, emphasizes that passion and perseverance for long-term goals often matter more than sheer talent. Caring deeply about your objective and refusing to give up can propel you further than you ever thought possible.

Actionable Strategies

A Growth Mindset Ninja knows grit is a muscle that can be developed with the **Four Cs**.

Confident: "I am confident when I visualize my success."
Take a moment each day to picture yourself achieving your goal, whether it's acing a test or finishing a marathon. Let that mental image fuel your belief in what's possible.

Calm: "I stay calm by using positive mantras like 'I can do this!'"
Stress is inevitable, but when you talk kindly to yourself, you lower anxiety and boost motivation. A simple, repeated phrase can help you refocus during tough moments.

Carefree: "I feel carefree when I face my fear of failure. I do this by asking, 'What's the worst thing that can happen?' Then I answer it. Next, I ask, 'Will I survive?'"
By tackling the possibility of failure head-on, you often realize it's not as scary as you imagined. Confronting your fears can help you loosen up, breathe, and keep going, free from the heavy weight of "what if?"

Capable: "I am capable of creating and achieving goals."
A Growth Mindset Ninja knows that success isn't just about raw talent. It's about setting targets, working steadily, and believing that you can master new skills. Capability grows with practice and patience.

Now that we've laid out the 4 Cs for building grit, let's dive into some everyday teen scenarios where you can see these principles in action.

Relatable Scenarios

Scenario 1: Sports Tryout Disappointment

You tried out for varsity basketball but only made JV. Lean on your Four Cs. Visualize yourself improving (Confident), repeat "I can do this!" (Calm), recognize it's okay to fail before succeeding (Carefree), and set a goal to practice daily (Capable).

Scenario 2: Heavy Homework Load

Midterms are looming, and you feel swamped. Grit reminds you to break tasks into chunks. Stay calm and trust that you can handle each chapter one at a time.

Scenario 3: Learning a New Instrument

The squeaks and squawks of the early days can be discouraging. But each little improvement, mastering a note, playing a scale, proves you're more than able to overcome obstacles.

"**It's** not that I'm so smart, it's just that I stay with problems longer." – Albert Einstein

Personal Story: Cross-Country

I still remember the day I signed up for the cross-country team in ninth grade, my grand plan was to jog a little, make friends, and look effortlessly sporty while doing it. How hard could running be, right? Spoiler alert: *very hard.*

On my first day of practice, I tried to keep up with my teammates, who all seemed to glide across the track like gazelles in a nature documentary. Meanwhile, I was huffing, puffing, and sweating in places I didn't know could sweat. I think at one point I might've left a lung on the field, my memory's hazy. By the week's end, I was the last to finish every run, my legs felt like pudding, and I was seriously considering faking an ankle sprain (or maybe a bad case of the sniffles) to avoid further humiliation.

My coach, however, had a sixth sense for picking up on potential quitters. One day, after I'd practically crawled across the finish line, he patted me on the shoulder and said, "Everyone starts somewhere. Stick with it." Right then, I realized maybe I didn't have to morph into an Olympic sprinter overnight, I just had to *keep going.* So I decided to give the "grit" thing a try, armed with a few mind tricks I'd picked up from friends, YouTube, and one too many motivational posters.

- Confident: I started imagining myself crossing the finish line like a champion, maybe even throwing in a victory fist-pump for extra flair. That mental picture kept me going when my calves were screaming "STOP, PLEASE!"
- Calm: Whenever I felt a looming meltdown mid-run, I'd whisper "I can do this!" under my breath. I probably looked a little unhinged to bystanders, but hey, if it kept me from collapsing in a sweaty heap, I'd take it.
- Carefree: I realized the worst-case scenario was a slow time (or an unflattering finish-line photo). And guess what? That's not exactly a life-or-death catastrophe. Embracing the possibility of imperfection made each run a little less terrifying.

- Capable: With each practice, I chipped away at my mile time. One day, I noticed I wasn't lagging *as* far behind; maybe it was just five minutes behind the pack instead of ten. Progress is progress, right?

That's how the Four Cs turned me from a panting straggler into a motivated finisher. Let's be real: I never became the fastest runner on the team. There were still days I cursed the alarm clock, cursed the shoelaces that refused to stay tied, and definitely cursed any hill taller than a speed bump. But by the end of the season, I had shaved actual minutes off my time. One of my teammates, one of those graceful gazelles, joked that I'd graduated from "tortoise" to "slightly faster tortoise," which I took as the highest compliment imaginable.

Looking back, my cross-country journey was basically a highlight reel of embarrassing starts and triumphant finishes. I learned that grit, powered by confidence, calmness, a dash of carefree spirit, and the belief in my own capability, can push me further than I ever thought possible, literally and metaphorically. Now, whenever I face something daunting (like a huge exam or a karaoke night gone wrong), I think about those early morning runs, the feeling of borderline doom that gradually turned into determination, and the small personal records that meant the world to me.

If a once gasping, sweaty, everything-hurts me could find the will to keep pounding the track, then trust me, there's hope for you, too. Just lace up those metaphorical running shoes, channel your inner Growth Mindset Ninja, and remind yourself that every mile, every challenge, gets you one step closer to the finish line you once thought you'd never cross.

Case Study: The Unfinished Painting

Allison set out to create a detailed painting for an art contest, but frustration set in halfway as it didn't meet her lofty expectations.

Instead of scrapping it, she leaned on the Four Cs:

- She visualized the finished piece (Confident).
- Reminded herself "I can do this!" when anxiety bubbled up (Calm).
- Let go of the fear that it wouldn't be prize-worthy (Carefree).
- Broke the painting down into sections, focusing on one small area each day (Capable).

Allison finished on time, and while she didn't take first place, the judges praised her work for its unique style. More importantly, she felt proud for not giving up.

Quick Quiz Box

Which of the Four Cs can help you best when you're afraid to even start a project?

- A) Confident
- B) Calm
- C) Carefree
- D) Capable

(Answer: All of them, but if you had to pick one, Carefree can be crucial for overcoming the initial fear of failure.)

Journal Reflection Box

Think of a goal you've been avoiding. Which of the 4 Cs do you need the most right now, and why?

Action Challenge Chart

Goal / Challenge	Four Cs in Action	Outcome / Feeling
Raising a grade from C to B+	Visualize success; say 'I can do it' daily (Confident + Calm)	More motivated, less stressed
Trying out for a school play	Ask 'What's the worst that can happen?' (Carefree)	Excited to try, fear reduced
Saving for a new laptop	Plan a budget and set milestones (Capable)	Sense of control, progress

A Growth Mindset Ninja can overcome all things with a dash of confidence, a calm mind, a carefree approach to failure, and trust in our capabilities, we can overcome almost any hurdle life throws our way. So lace up those metaphorical sneakers and keep moving, because grit turns dreams into done!

Chapter 6 Key Takeaways

1. Grit > Raw Talent. Perseverance and consistency often outshine natural ability.
2. The 4 Cs. Be Confident, stay Calm, be Carefree about minor failures, and trust you're Capable.
3. Long Haul Mindset. True progress emerges from daily effort and resilience.

Mini-FAQ

Q1: What if I run out of motivation halfway through a project?
A: Revisit the 4 Cs. Visualize success (Confident) or remind yourself "I can do this" (Calm). Accept minor failures (Carefree). Set small goals to rebuild momentum (Capable).

Q2: When is it okay to quit?
A: Quitting isn't always bad if the goal truly no longer aligns with your interests or values. Just ensure it's a thoughtful decision, not panic or frustration. Sometimes reevaluating is part of grit! Persevering is great, but anger can derail you, let's learn to manage rage before it robs you of clear thinking.

7

CONTROLLING YOUR RAGE BEFORE IT CONTROLS YOU

Fury isn't just anger's bigger, scarier cousin, it's the kind of emotion that can turn even the calmest person into a full-blown volcano. While anger is normal, fury can be destructive if left unchecked, leading to damaged relationships, impulsive decisions, and major regret (like sending that all-caps text you *immediately* wish you could unsend).

Dr. Daniel Goleman, an emotional intelligence expert, explains that rage hijacks the brain's ability to think rationally. That's why, in the heat of the moment, it feels like the only option is to react *right now*, even when that reaction is absolutely not your best move. The secret? Recognizing the signs before fury takes the wheel. Practicing mindfulness, pausing, and taking control of your emotions allows you to respond rather than explode.

The good news? You don't have to let fury run the show. Learning how to manage extreme anger helps you keep your cool, avoid unnecessary blow-ups, and handle even the most frustrating situations with a clear mind, because let's be real, making decisions when you're furious usually leads to next-day regrets.

The Big Picture: Why Managing Anger Now Prepares You for Life

Let's be real, life will always have frustrating moments. Whether it's group projects, unfair decisions, rude people, or things just not going your way, anger is inevitable. But how you handle it now will shape the kind of person you become.

Think about it: The most successful people in the world, athletes, leaders, entrepreneurs, face criticism, rejection, and setbacks all the time. The ones who succeed aren't the ones who throw tantrums, they're the ones who stay calm, think clearly, and respond with strategy instead of rage.

If you can master anger management now, you're not just avoiding fights or regrets, you're building the skills to handle tough situations like a leader.

What Fury Feels Like in the Body

When fury takes over, your body goes into full-blown fight-or-flight mode, flooding you with stress hormones and preparing you to either fight a bear or flip a table (both of which are, let's be honest, *not great options*). Here's how it shows up:

- Rapid heartbeat & clenched fists – Your body is getting ready for a showdown, except the only enemy is your own frustration.
- Tight jaw & tense muscles – Because apparently, your shoulders think they need to be up near your ears when you're mad.
- Tunnel vision & difficulty thinking clearly – Your brain zooms in on the problem and completely forgets logic, reason, and sometimes even basic words.
- Shaky hands & short, fast breaths – Your body gears up for battle, but instead of helping, it just makes you look like you've had way too much caffeine.

The Bigger Picture: Why Anger Management is a Life Skill

Mastering your anger isn't just about avoiding fights, it's about learning to handle conflict, stay in control, and make smart decisions. Here's how it benefits you:
- Better Communication – Instead of yelling or shutting down, you can express what's bothering you clearly(which makes people actually listen to you!).
- Stronger Relationships – Managing anger helps you avoid unnecessary fights and keeps friendships, family, and work relationships strong.
- Improved Decision-Making – When you're calm under pressure, you make better choices, which leads to fewer regrets.
- More Respect from Others – People respect those who can stay composed and handle conflict maturely (trust me, no one respects a hothead).

The Bottom Line? Don't Let Fury Make Your Decisions

Fury feels powerful in the moment, but if you don't take control, it takes control of you. Learning to recognize when you're about to explode, stepping back, and using mindfulness techniques can be the difference between resolving an issue or making it way worse. And let's be real, handling anger like a pro is way more impressive than flipping out.

Expert Advice

Dr. Ray Novaco, a clinical psychologist, emphasizes the importance of anger regulation. He advises using self-talk techniques, such as saying, *I am in control, and I can handle this calmly*, to regain power over emotions.

Actionable Strategies

A Growth Mindset Ninja follows the C.A.L.M. strategy to stay in control:

C – Count to 10 – Give your brain time to think before reacting.

A – Allow Yourself to Feel All the Feelings – Say to yourself, *I feel upset, and that's okay, but I can control how I respond.*

L – Listen to Your Body – Notice how your body feels and take deep breaths to relax.

M – Make a Positive Choice – Choose a calm response instead of letting your anger take over.

Other techniques include:

- Cooling Off: Splash cold water on your face or take a short walk.
- Talking It Out: Express your feelings with someone you trust instead of bottling them up.
- Physical Release: Try activities like running, hitting a punching bag, or deep stretching to release built-up tension.

Try these techniques and see how managing fury helps you stay in control and find better solutions!

Relatable Scenarios

Scenario 1: Someone Spreads a Rumor About You

You walk into school and hear people whispering. A friend tells you that someone started a false rumor about you. Your face burns with anger, and your first thought is, *I'm going to call them out in front of everyone!* You feel like yelling or sending an angry text to defend yourself.

Reframing the Thought: Instead of reacting immediately, you take a few deep breaths and think before acting. You remind yourself, *Lashing out will only make things worse.* You calmly confront the person privately and let them know the truth. By staying in control of your emotions, you protect your reputation without escalating the drama.

Scenario 2: Getting Benched in a Game

You've been working hard in practice, but when game day comes, the coach benches you. You feel humiliated and furious, especially when you see a teammate who doesn't work as hard getting more playtime. *This isn't fair! What's the point of trying?*

Reframing the Thought: Instead of letting anger take over, you remind yourself, *I can use this as motivation.* You talk to your coach after practice and ask what you can do to improve. By turning frustration into determination, you push yourself to work harder and prove you deserve a spot on the field.

Scenario 3: A Teacher Blames You for Something You Didn't Do

During class, a teacher accuses you of talking when it was actually the person next to you. You feel your fists clench, your heart race, and the words *That's not fair!* are on the tip of your tongue.

Reframing the Thought: Instead of snapping back in frustration, you take a deep breath and wait until after class to explain the situation calmly. The teacher apologizes for the mistake, and you realize that staying in control of your emotions helped resolve the situation peacefully.

Scenario 4: Someone Disrespects Someone You Care About

You're walking through the hallway when you overhear someone making fun of your friend. You feel instant rage, your friend doesn't deserve that! Your first instinct is to confront them aggressively and make them regret it.

Reframing the Thought: Instead of letting fury take over, you remind yourself: *I can stand up for my friend without making things worse.* You approach the situation calmly, let the person know their words aren't okay, and check in on your friend to make sure they feel supported.

"**Speak** when you are angry, and you'll make the best speech you'll ever regret." — Ambrose Bierce

Personal Story

When I was younger, I had a short temper, especially when I felt disrespected or treated unfairly. I wasn't the type to stay quiet when something upset me. If I felt wronged, I reacted immediately, sometimes with yelling, snapping back, or storming off. But one experience taught me a powerful lesson about how to control fury before it controls you.

One day at school, I had worked really hard on a group project. I stayed up late, did extra research, and made sure everything was perfect. But when it was time to present, one of my group members took all the credit, acting like they had done the majority of the work. The teacher praised them, and I sat there, boiling inside.

Are you kidding me? I did most of the work! My face burned with anger. My hands clenched into fists under my desk. I wanted to call them out in front of the whole class, to make sure everyone knew the truth.

But then, I heard my mom's voice in my head: *Anger makes you reactive, wisdom makes you effective.* I knew that if I exploded in the moment, I'd only look out of control, and nothing would get fixed. So instead, I took deep breaths and waited until after class.

Once I had calmed down, I pulled my teacher aside and explained what really happened. Instead of reacting in anger, I used logic and stated the facts. My teacher listened, apologized for not realizing it earlier, and made sure the grades were adjusted fairly. If I had lashed out in class, I wouldn't have gotten that outcome.

That experience changed how I saw fury. I realized that anger itself isn't bad, it's a signal that something feels unfair or wrong. But how we respond to that anger determines whether we solve the problem or make it worse. I learned that true strength isn't just about speaking up, it's about knowing when and how to do it wisely.

To this day, I remind myself: *It's okay to feel anger, but don't let it decide your next move.*

Case Study: The Locker Room Clash

Dante's temper got the best of him when his teammate blamed him for losing the game. Instead of throwing his water bottle like a dramatic sports movie villain, he walked away, cooled off, and later talked it out. He realized that real strength wasn't about winning arguments, it was about knowing when to let go and move forward.

Quick Quiz Box

What's the best way to handle extreme anger?

- a) Take deep breaths and step away
- b) Yell to let it all out
- c) Act on impulse immediately
- d) Hold it in until it goes away

(Answer: a) Take deep breaths and step away)

Journal Reflection Box

Write about a time you felt furious. What triggered it? How did you react? What could you do differently next time?

Action Challenge Chart

Trigger	Initial Reaction	New Calm Response
Someone insults me	Yell back	Walk away and address it later
Lose a game unfairly	Slam my fist down	Take deep breaths and reframe my thinking
Get blamed for something I didn't do	Argue immediately	Explain my side calmly

Chapter 7 Key Takeaways

Anger is a normal emotion, it's how you handle it that matters. Pausing before reacting helps prevent regretful outbursts. Channeling anger into healthy outlets leads to better outcomes.

Mini-FAQ

Q1: What if I can't stop myself from exploding?
A: Use the C.A.L.M. method, Count to 10, Acknowledge feelings, Let it out safely, Make a plan.

Q2: Is anger always bad?
A: No! Anger can be productive when used to set boundaries, advocate for yourself, or push for positive change.

With fury under control, next we'll tackle how to flow like water when life takes unexpected turns.

8

FLOWING WITH LIFE'S CHANGES

Picture this: you've got your entire day planned down to the minute, homework at 4:00, snack break at 4:45, gaming at 5:00, dinner at 6:00, only to have it all go *poof* because your mom needs a hand with groceries or your teacher drops a last-minute project on you. If your initial reaction is to rage internally or crumble into a meltdown, you know just how unsettling change can be. Adaptability is about rolling with those interruptions, turning unexpected twists into opportunities rather than miniature disasters.

In a world that updates faster than your phone's operating system, learning to pivot gracefully saves you a truckload of stress. After all, not everything can (or should) go exactly as planned. A Growth Mindset Ninja sees obstacles as detours worth exploring, sometimes, the wrong turn leads to an accidental adventure you'll talk about for weeks.

- Reduces Stress: When you can change gears smoothly, surprises feel less catastrophic.
- Encourages Creativity: Adapting often means coming up with new ideas on the fly, hello, out-of-the-box thinking!

- Strengthens Relationships: Friends, family, and group partners appreciate someone who can bend without breaking.

Adaptability doesn't mean you never struggle; it means you acknowledge change is inevitable, and you decide to dance with it instead of fight it.

Different Flavors of (In)Flexibility

Not all inflexibility is the same. You might spot yourself in one or more categories:

1. The Schedule Die-Hard
   » If anything or anyone messes with your precious timetable, you feel like flipping a table. You cling to your plan like it's the only path forward.
2. The Control Enthusiast
   » You have a crystal-clear vision of how tasks must be done (usually your way). Deviations make you anxious or irritated.
3. The Comfort-Zone Camper
   » You prefer tried-and-true routines. The second someone suggests a new approach or location, you recoil like a snail tapped on the shell.
4. The Panic Planner
   » You try to plan for every worst-case scenario in advance. When real life doesn't match your predictions, you're left reeling.Recognizing which type of "I hate change" you exhibit is the first step toward letting go, letting events unfold in ways you can't always script.

The Sneaky Consequences of "Change Freak-Out"

When you resist every pivot, you may not realize how it quietly chips away at your happiness:

- Sky-High Stress: Clinging to rigid expectations sets you up for disappointment whenever reality, inevitably, doesn't comply.
- Missed Opportunities: If you're too busy lamenting that Plan A failed, you might overlook the cooler Plan B waiting in the wings.
- Strained Relationships: Insisting everything go your way can drive friends and family up the wall, nobody likes feeling micromanaged or at fault for "ruining" your plan.
- Delayed Problem-Solving: Instead of finding quick workarounds, you spend time fuming that the original approach didn't pan out.
- Anxiety Over the Unknown: Inflexibility feeds the fear of "what if?" until it morphs into a full-blown dread of trying anything new.

Uncontrolled inflexibility is like wearing blinders, you miss the unexpected shortcuts, joys, and small wonders that pop up when you allow life some wiggle room.

How It Applies in Real Life / How It Affects You in Life

- Group Projects: If a team member can't finish their part, you can either melt down or pivot, maybe rearrange tasks or find a new presentation angle.
- Friendships: People grow and change. Being adaptable allows you to maintain friendships even when life pulls you in new directions.
- Future Goals: Don't let a single path define you. Adaptable folks thrive because they see possibilities in every turn of the journey.

What Resistance to Change Feels Like in the Body

Just like any emotional tension, your body has ways of letting you know when you're struggling with adaptability:

- Tense Muscles: Shoulders hunched up around your ears, neck stiff, or hands clenched. It's like your body's bracing for a fight.
- Knotted Stomach: That uneasy swirl can appear the moment you sense something's not going according to plan.
- Quickened Pulse or Shallow Breathing: Your system interprets unexpected changes as threats, flipping your stress response to ON.
- Restlessness: An inflexible mind can make you feel jittery or unsettled when your routine is thrown off.
- Irritability: Internal frustration sometimes leaks out as snappy comments or a hair-trigger temper.

If you notice these signals whenever a change rolls in, it's a sign your body is tensing up against the current, like trying to swim upstream when the river is flowing the other way.

Ready to see how a Growth Mindset Ninja transforms "This is *not* how I planned it!" into "Huh, maybe this detour's worth exploring"? Next, we'll dive into expert advice and actionable strategies that'll help you become more flexible (without losing your sense of direction). Because who knows, sometimes Plan B (or C, or D) might be more memorable than the script you wrote in your head.

Expert Advice

Organizational and developmental psychologists often emphasize the importance of "cognitive flexibility", the ability to switch thinking modes or perspectives. It's a hallmark of successful problem-solvers, from entrepreneurs to artists.

Actionable Strategies

A Growth Mindset Ninja **flows like water**.

1. **Observe the Current**
    - » Take a moment to notice what's really going on. If a change disrupts your plan, pause and gather the facts,

like water testing which way the stream flows before moving on.

2. **Stay Fluid**
   - » Water adjusts to its container; likewise, let yourself adapt to the new circumstances. This might mean revising your schedule, altering your approach, or brainstorming fresh solutions.

3. **Go Around Obstacles**
   - » When water hits a rock, it flows around it instead of trying to break straight through. If you encounter a roadblock, like a canceled event or a resource shortage, ask yourself, *How else can I reach my goal?*

4. **Embrace Change**
   - » Water doesn't fear transformation (liquid, ice, vapor). Lean into changes instead of viewing them as threats. Each shift can be an opportunity to learn or discover something unexpected.

Now that you know how to "flow like water," let's explore some everyday teen scenarios where adaptability transforms unexpected obstacles into fresh opportunities.

Relatable Scenarios

Scenario 1: Last-Minute Class Switch

You planned your schedule around a certain teacher, but you get switched to another class. Flow like water: observe the new class vibe, find classmates to connect with, and adapt study methods if needed.

Scenario 2: Canceled Hangout

Your friend bails at the last second. Rather than sulk, pivot to solo adventures, maybe a bike ride, a new recipe, or starting that art project you've been eyeing.

Scenario 3: Tech Trouble

Your laptop dies mid-assignment. Instead of panicking, see if you can borrow a device or work from your phone for research. Adapt to the constraint rather than letting it freeze your progress.

"**You** must be shapeless, formless, like water."
– Bruce Lee

Personal Story: The Big Move

I still remember the day my mom announced we'd be moving to a new city, right smack in the middle of freshman year. It felt like someone had yanked the rug out from under my carefully assembled routine: I had a solid friend group, a beloved locker location right next to the cafeteria (prime real estate!), and a daily after-school hang with my besties where we'd tear through snacks and gossip about everything from school drama to the latest superhero movies.

Suddenly, poof, my schedule, my friends, and my once-upon-a-time daydreams of finishing high school in the same place vanished into cardboard boxes. I had zero choice but to pack up my life, wave goodbye to all that was familiar, and haul my entire existence (including a suspiciously large collection of plushies) to some unknown town. Cue the epic "doom music" in my head.

Stepping into my new school felt like being dropped into a foreign country without a map or a phrasebook. I had to figure out who was friendly, which hallways led to the cafeteria instead of the boiler room, and how to stay afloat in classes that used different textbooks than my old school. My first day, I got lost three times, tripped over a loose tile in front of an entire table of upperclassmen, and managed to forget my lunch at home. By the time the final bell rang, I was two parts overwhelmed and one part starving.

But funny enough, my accidental detours led me to discover new corners of school I wouldn't have seen otherwise, like the super-cozy reading nook in the library and a hallway plastered with art club projects. One day, while I was searching (again) for the main office, I stumbled across a door labeled "Creative Writing Club meets here." On a whim, I stuck my head in. A junior with bright pink hair waved me over, inviting me to join them as they brainstormed story ideas. Within minutes, I was laughing at their goofy inside jokes and sharing some of my own doodles and random short stories. It was like finding a secret society of fellow nerds who spoke my language.

As I navigated the next few weeks, I realized adaptability was less about magically loving every new thing and more about keeping myself open to unexpected upsides. Sure, I missed my old friends like crazy, I even wrote a poem or two about it for the Creative Writing Club. But I also started to see that my new environment had quirks I could appreciate. My teachers turned out to be pretty fun once I got past that initial "Uh, who are you?" awkwardness, and a couple of friendly classmates introduced me to a local café that served the best hot chocolate I'd ever tasted.

Yes, there were still days I felt out of place or wished I could teleport back to my old life. Like when I heard about some big event my old friends were going to, or when I messed up my schedule trying to switch classes. But piece by piece, I found new routines. I had new lunch buddies, one who shared my love of 90s pop music (don't judge, we vibe), and another who roped me into the film club's mission to record random campus antics for a year-end montage. They even convinced me to appear on-camera a couple of times, me being "the new kid giving a campus tour," which was hilariously ironic since I still got lost occasionally.

The biggest surprise was how soon I started calling this new school "ours." Once I stopped resisting every change, I realized it wasn't all that different from my old place, just some fresh personalities, hallways, and traditions. Over time, my nerves settled, my sense of humor returned, and I felt comfortable enough to bust out my corny jokes in creative writing sessions. (They kindly let me live down the truly terrible puns.)

Looking back, I see that the move forced me to adapt in ways I never anticipated, like learning to scan a map of campus in my head, forging new friendships from scratch, and figuring out that yes, I can handle lunches alone until I meet the right group (thank you, good books on my e-reader). In a weird twist, my biggest meltdown moments, getting lost, missing lunch, popping into an unknown club, opened doors I never expected to see.

So, while I wouldn't exactly volunteer to move mid-year all over again, I'd be lying if I said it was all bad. In fact, it turned out to be an eye-opening adventure. Adapting taught me that new

> places and people might be awkward at first, but they can also lead to random joys and experiences I'd miss if I stuck to my comfort zone. And if anything, I gained a killer sense of direction, or at least I can now confidently say, "You're looking for the art hallway? Let me show you!" without winding up in the boiler room again.

Case Study: The Unplanned Art Project

Carmen spent hours meticulously designing a painting for a local art show. The night before it was due, her paintbrush snapped, and she couldn't get a new one in time. Instead of admitting defeat, she grabbed a sponge and some old rags, layering paint in unique textures. Her painting ended up more striking than she'd imagined, her spontaneity impressed the show judges, and she got an honorable mention. Go, Growth Mindset Ninja vibes!

Quick Quiz Box

Which of the following best shows an "adaptable" response when your friend can't make it to the movies?

- A) Cancel your day and wallow in disappointment
- B) Text them angrily about how they ruined your entire week
- C) Flow like water: find a different friend to go with or plan a fun solo activity
- D) Binge negative social media posts to match your mood

(Answer: C. That's the Flow Like Water way, pivot and embrace new possibilities.)

Journal Reflection Box

Write about a time when your plans fell apart. How did you handle it? If you could rewind, where could you apply "flow like water" to adapt more smoothly?

Action Challenge Chart

Unexpected Twist	Flow Like Water Step	Outcome / Feeling
Study partner no-show	Observed a new way to review alone	Learned to create your own practice quiz
Teacher changes the assignment last-minute	Stayed fluid with ideas for the new prompt	Less stress, discovered a more creative angle
Family trip rerouted	Went around obstacles by scheduling different activities	Gained fresh experiences, new memories

    A Growth Mindset Ninja proves that when you "flow like water," you won't just survive life's twists, you'll thrive. By staying fluid, embracing change, and looking for the path around each obstacle, you transform challenges into stepping stones on your epic journey forward!

Chapter 8 Key Takeaways

1. Life Shifts Constantly. Being adaptable reduces stress and fosters creativity.
2. Flow Like Water. Observe, Stay fluid, Go around obstacles, Embrace change.
3. Detours Can Be Gold. Sometimes Plan B or C becomes the best story.

Mini-FAQ

Q1: What if I just hate unexpected changes altogether?
A: Start small: plan an "unplanned" day where you let events unfold. Notice that life doesn't implode; you might discover hidden perks. Think of it as practice in letting go.

Q2: People say I'm indecisive when I 'flow like water.' How do I respond?
A: Adapting doesn't mean lacking direction, explain you're flexible, not aimless. You still have goals, you're just open to new paths if the first one hits a snag.

Adapting gracefully is essential, but a negative mindset can still sabotage you, prepare to flip withdrawals into deposits.

9

SHIFTING FROM WITHDRAWALS TO DEPOSITS

Have you ever caught yourself thinking, *"I'll probably fail anyway,"* or, "No one cares what I have to say"? That little storm cloud perched on your shoulder, that's negativity. It can show up as self-doubt, pessimistic predictions, or an unending stream of harsh self-talk. Sure, some skepticism can keep us realistic, but when negativity runs wild, it drowns out hope, confidence, and all the good stuff that keeps us going.

A Growth Mindset Ninja knows that we don't have to believe every critical thought crossing our minds. While negativity might feel like it's "protecting" you from disappointment, it often blocks you from growth, new experiences, and feeling good about yourself. Over time, that relentless voice can turn small hiccups into full-blown doom scenarios, unless you learn to tame it.

- Self-Confidence Booster: Curbing negative self-talk can clear the way for healthy confidence.
- Improved Relationships: If you're not always expecting the worst, you're more open and approachable to friends and family.
- Better Overall Mood: Duh, less negativity means more room for fun, curiosity, and celebrating the small joys in life.

Different Flavors of Negativity

Negativity can wear a variety of masks, see if any of these ring a bell:

1. The Worst-Case Scenario Guru
   - » You predict every possible disaster, from flunking a test to alien-invasion-level catastrophes. No matter the situation, you're already mourning its failure.
2. The "I'm Not Good Enough" Parrot
   - » Like a broken record, you tell yourself you're not smart, talented, or likable, over and over, until you half-believe it's fact.
3. The Cynic-in-Chief
   - » If something nice happens, you immediately suspect a catch. Compliments? Must be fake. Success? Clearly a fluke.
4. The Drama Amplifier
   - » Small issues balloon into Titanic-level calamities. A tiny disagreement or a single bad grade means your entire day, week, even life, is ruined.

Sometimes, negativity stems from protective instincts, like not wanting to get your hopes up. Other times, it's just a habit, one that can spiral if we don't hit the brakes.

The Sneaky Consequences of Uncontrolled Negativity

When negativity hijacks your mindset, it can quietly meddle with all aspects of life:

- Low Self-Esteem: Constantly trash-talking yourself leaves you feeling worthless or incompetent.
- Stressed-Out Relationships: You might assume friends are judging you or interpret harmless jokes as personal attacks.
- Missed Opportunities: If you expect everything to flop, you're less likely to try new clubs, sports, or even open up to new friendships.

- Anxiety & Depression: Negative thinking can worsen or trigger mental health struggles, feeding into a cycle that's tough to break.
- Chronic Gloom: Over time, negativity can drain color from everyday life, making even good moments feel "meh." Sometimes, negativity can trick you into thinking it's keeping you safe. In reality, it's often the mental equivalent of pouring cold water on every spark of excitement or confidence.

How It Applies in Real Life / How It Affects You in Life

- Friendships: If you always assume friends will let you down, you might push them away or avoid making plans.
- Family: Negative comments can erode trust over time, making even casual disagreements feel like huge blowouts.
- Classmates & Teams: In group projects, negativity can cause tension, dragging down morale and productivity.

What Negativity Feels Like in the Body

Yep, this mental habit can have physical side effects:

- Knotted Stomach: Negative thoughts can cause a low-level churn of anxiety almost all day.
- Muscle Tension: Shoulders practically glued to your ears, jaw clenched, your body acts like it's bracing for disaster.
- Fatigue: Mentally battling yourself can be exhausting, leaving you drained and unmotivated.
- Shallow Breathing: Pessimistic thoughts can trigger mild stress responses, making you breathe in short, quick bursts.
- Headaches or Migraines: Chronic tension and stress can lead to nagging headaches that just won't quit.

Your body's basically sending out distress signals, saying, "Hey, this negativity is wearing us down, mind giving us a break?"

Ready to see how a Growth Mindset Ninja swaps out nagging "I can't" and "I'll fail" beliefs for a more balanced, hopeful outlook?

Up next, we'll explore expert advice and actionable strategies to redirect that gloomy train onto a sunnier track, because life's too short to spend every moment waiting for catastrophe.

Expert Advice

Stephen R. Covey popularized the concept of the Emotional Bank Account, explaining that positive interactions (like honesty, empathy, and keeping promises) are "deposits," while negative interactions (like disrespect, criticism, or broken promises) act as "withdrawals." Keep more deposits than withdrawals, and your relationships flourish, whether with friends, teachers, family, or even yourself.

Actionable Strategies

A Growth Mindset Ninja understands how to make deposits into accounts and limits withdrawals.

1. **Recognize the "Balance"**
   » Each relationship has its own Emotional Bank Account. Think of trust and goodwill as currency. If you're often critical or distant, you're withdrawing from that account.
2. **Make Deposits**
   » Kind Words & Gestures: Simple compliments, genuine apologies, or offering help can add up.
   » Keep Promises: Following through on what you say you'll do is a huge deposit, consistency builds trust.
   » Listen Actively: Give someone your full attention, even if it's just for a few minutes.
3. **Limit Withdrawals**
   » Check Your Tone: Sarcasm or harshness can subtract from the account, even if you didn't mean it that way.
   » Avoid Snap Judgments: Hearing the full story before reacting prevents unnecessary conflict.
   » Address Issues Carefully: Criticism is sometimes needed, but deliver it with respect and solutions rather than blame.
4. **Monitor Your Own Account**

> Notice how you feel about yourself. Negative self-talk is like making withdrawals from your own Emotional Bank Account. Show some self-compassion, deposit kindness toward yourself, too!

Now that you understand how Emotional Bank Accounts operate, let's see how these strategies play out in everyday teen scenarios.

Relatable Scenarios

Scenario 1: Group Chat Dilemmas

You miss a couple of messages and assume everyone's ignoring you (negative mindset). Instead, deposit trust: ask politely if something came up, and keep communication open.

Scenario 2: Team Sports Woes

You're worried teammates will judge you for a bad play. Rather than snapping at them, deposit positivity by asking for advice or offering support when they slip up, too.

Scenario 3: Family Conflicts

Arguments at home can drain everyone's Emotional Bank Account if negativity rules. Focus on calm words, active listening, and respectful boundaries to rebuild trust.

"**Trust** is the glue of life. It's the most essential ingredient in effective communication. It's the foundational principle that holds all relationships."
– Stephen R. Covey

Personal Story

I realized I'd turned into a chronic complainer when my best friend said, "Dude, you're so negative," and I brushed her off, proving her point. School stress plus low energy made me snap at my sister, roll my eyes at my parents, and ghost my friends.

Then I recalled a concept called the Emotional Bank Account: every action is either a deposit (positive, trust-building) or a withdrawal (negative, trust-eroding). After a big blowup with my mom over a simple request, I realized I was deep in the red with everyone around me.

I decided to reverse course by making deposits:

- **Start Small at Home**: Actually listen to my mom's day, compliment my sister's art, keep sarcasm in check.
- **Reach Out to Friends**: Apologize for pulling away, plan a gaming night, replace grumbling with gratitude.

It felt forced at first, but I saw immediate changes, my family relaxed, my sister showed me her art again, and my best friend and I had fun without my negativity overshadowing it. Over time, those small positive "deposits" built trust back up.

Now I try to watch my words, offer genuine kindness, and apologize quickly when I slip. I'm not perfect, but focusing on making deposits instead of withdrawals has boosted my relationships, and my own mood. It turns out expecting nothing but the worst just leads to isolation, while simple acts of caring reconnect me with the people who matter most.

Case Study: The "Lunch Table Letdown"

Rylie often groaned about how her friends never invited her to hang out, blaming them for being "fake." But she also rarely took the initiative to ask them out or plan anything fun, stacking up negative assumptions. When a new friend explained the Emotional Bank

Account concept, Rylie realized her negativity was a withdrawal. She started inviting them to sit with her at lunch (deposit), sent encouraging texts when they had tough tests (deposit), and gently asked if she could come along on weekend outings (deposit). Little by little, the trust balance grew, and she felt truly included.

Quick Quiz Box

Which action is a "deposit" to someone's Emotional Bank Account?

- A) Making fun of a friend's outfit
- B) Promising to help with a task but backing out last minute
- C) Complimenting them sincerely on a recent achievement
- D) Ignoring messages and refusing to explain why

(Answer: C. A sincere compliment is a positive deposit into trust and goodwill.)

Journal Reflection Box

Identify a relationship in your life that feels strained. Which deposits can you make this week to rebuild trust? What withdrawals do you need to cut back on?

Action Challenge Chart

Relationship	Deposit Action	Outcome / Feeling
Classmate I argued with	Apologize and ask if they need help with homework	Reopened communication, less tension
Parent I rarely talk to	Share one good thing about my day daily	Built warmth, more relaxed talks
Myself (negative self-talk)	Catch & replace harsh inner comments with kinder thoughts	Reduced stress, felt more confident

A Growth Mindset Ninja understands that negativity can become a default setting, but it doesn't have to stay that way. By viewing each relationship (including the one with yourself) as an Emotional Bank Account, you can consciously choose deposits of trust, kindness, and support, and watch negativity shift into positivity and connection.

Chapter 9 Key Takeaways

1. Negativity Drains Trust. Each interaction can be a deposit (positive) or withdrawal (negative).
2. Aim for More Deposits. Compliments, promises kept, genuine listening.
3. Self-Talk Matters. Negative inner dialogue is a withdrawal from your emotional bank, too.

Mini-FAQ

Q1: What if my negativity feels 'justified' because life is rough right now?

A: Stress happens, but piling negativity onto friends or family can burn bridges. Start small: find one positive statement or small gratitude each day. You can be real about struggles while still offering kindness.

Q2: How do I deal with people who always make *me* feel negative?
A: Sometimes you may need boundary-setting or gentle honesty. Share how their negativity affects you. If they won't change, focus on protecting your emotional balance with healthy self-talk and leaning on supportive folks.

You've replaced negativity with trust; now let's embrace the real you, free from masks or apologies.

10

EMBRACING THE 4 Ls

Ever felt like you had to wear a mask just to fit in, pretending to love a TV show you actually find boring, or acting super confident when inside, you're practically screaming? That's where authenticity (or lack thereof) comes into play. Being authentic isn't about spilling every detail of your life to everyone you meet; it's about feeling comfortable enough in your own skin that you don't need to change who you are for anyone else's approval.

A Growth Mindset Ninja reminds us that it's okay to have quirks and preferences that don't align with the crowd. Sure, sometimes you might tweak your behavior to avoid hurting someone's feelings or follow social norms, but if you're constantly suppressing your true thoughts, interests, or personality, you end up living someone else's script, not your own.

- Fosters Self-Respect: You learn to like, if not love, the person you see in the mirror, because that person is *you*, not a fabricated version.
- Builds Genuine Connections: True friendships form when people connect with the real you, not a costume you wear to impress them.

- Boosts Emotional Health: Authentic living lowers stress by killing the constant worry of *"What if they find out who I really am?"*

When you let your true self shine, even if it feels scary at first, you'll discover there's a whole world of people who appreciate you for exactly who you are.

Different Ways We Hide Our True Selves

Not all "inauthentic" behavior is obvious. You might relate to one or more of these:

1. The Social Chameleon
   » You adapt your likes and dislikes depending on the crowd. If your friends love a band, you pretend to love it too, though you can't name a single song.
2. The Over-Polite Agree-er
   » You nod along with everyone's ideas to avoid conflict, even when you secretly disagree or have your own opinions burning to get out.
3. The Social Media Curator
   » Your online persona is super outgoing or artsy, but in reality, you rarely engage in those big, bold hobbies, yet you keep posting for the "aesthetic."
4. The "Everything's Fine" Actor
   » You bury your emotions behind a permanent smile, scared people won't accept your frustrations, sadness, or vulnerability.

Sometimes, blending in can help you navigate new situations, but if it becomes your default, you risk losing touch with what you truly value, love, or think.

The Sneaky Consequences of Living Inauthentically

Pretending to be someone you're not might seem harmless at first, until you see the ripple effect:

- Chronic Stress: Constantly performing a role wears you down. You're always checking if your "act" is convincing, which can lead to mental and emotional fatigue.
- Shallow Relationships: If you're not letting people see the real you, how can they truly connect with you? That can leave you feeling lonely in a crowd.
- Self-Doubt: Faking it can erode your self-confidence. You might start questioning your own likes, talents, or even your worth, uncertain which parts are genuine.
- Anxiety Over "Exposure": The fear of someone discovering your secret fandom, your real feelings, or your true personality can create a constant sense of unease.
- Missed Opportunities: Authentic interests and passions might never bloom if you're too busy trying to fit a mold. Constantly faking it leads to confusion about your own preferences.

In short, living in-authentically means you're always tiptoeing around a version of yourself that isn't real. It's exhausting and blocks the chance for genuine growth and happiness.

What Inauthentic Living Feels Like in the Body

Pretending or hiding your true self can trigger a surprising physical toll:

- Tension Headaches: Stress from keeping up appearances can cause your muscles to tighten, especially around your neck and temples.
- Knotted Stomach: Feeling like you're living a lie can manifest as that queasy, anxious churn in your gut.

- Uneasy Breathing: If you're constantly in "performance" mode, shallow, quick breaths might become your norm, like your body's bracing for an emotional ambush.
- Shoulder/Neck Tightness: Lying or omitting parts of who you are can translate into carrying tension up in your shoulders, leaving you sore at the end of the day.
- Exhaustion: Masking your real thoughts and feelings chews through mental and emotional resources, leaving you drained when you finally get some alone time.

Your body's basically telling you, "Hey, this performance is wearing us out, can we just be ourselves, please?"

Curious to see how a Growth Mindset Ninja unlocks the best parts of being unapologetically you? Up next, we'll explore expert advice and actionable strategies to help you shed the masks, embrace your quirks, and connect with the world on your own terms. Because life's too short to live as someone you aren't, and far more rewarding when you let your real self shine.

Expert Advice

Psychologists highlight that self-congruence, living in harmony with your authentic self, boosts overall mental health. People who act in line with their core beliefs are often happier, more resilient, and experience stronger connections in their relationships.

Actionable Strategies

A Growth Mindset Ninja practices the **Four Ls** to tap into their authenticity.

Listen to My Heart
» Tune out the noise for a moment and ask yourself: What do I truly feel? Whether it's excitement, doubt, or curiosity, acknowledging your real emotions is the first step toward authenticity.

Love Myself
- » Self-kindness is non-negotiable. Embrace your quirks, celebrate small wins, and be gentle when you slip up. Loving yourself fuels your confidence and helps you bounce back from mistakes.

Live My Truth
- » Speak and act in ways that reflect your real identity, interests, and values. If you love reading fantasy novels, don't be shy about discussing them, even if it's not "popular." Your truth is your superpower.

Lean on Others
- » Being authentic doesn't mean going it alone. Seek out supportive friends, mentors, or family members who appreciate the real you. Ask for help when you need it and offer the same in return.

Now that you've learned how the Four Ls can help you stay true to yourself, let's explore some real-life situations where authenticity makes all the difference.

Relatable Scenarios

Scenario 1: Choosing Extracurriculars

If all your friends join the debate team, but your heart's in the drama club, following it is a great way to Live Your Truth.

Scenario 2: Dealing with Peer Pressure

When everyone's raving about a new trend, Listen to Your Heart: do you actually like it, or are you just afraid of being left out? If it's not your vibe, loving yourself means you can say, "Thanks, but I'll pass."

Scenario 3: Exploring Future Goals

Lean on Others, like a trusted teacher or counselor, to talk through your real interests, maybe you want to try culinary school instead of business. Listening to your heart here could be life-changing.

"**Be** yourself; everyone else is already taken."
– Oscar Wilde

Personal Story: The Time I Almost Fell for a Scam

Junior year, I was juggling National Honor Society, cross-country, and pom-poms, part bookworm, part glitter-loving girl. At my old lunch table, I felt like a misfit, too nervous to share my real interests. One day, after a particularly dull conversation about the latest gossip, I got up, tray shaking, and marched to a different table.

This new group was a joyful mix of "misfits": a girl from chem class who loved creative writing, another who scribbled art during lunch, and a cross-country teammate I'd barely known. They welcomed me instantly, scooting over to make room. When I introduced myself as a "writing nerd who also loves science," nobody blinked. Instead, someone said, "Awesome! Tell me more." Suddenly, I found people who actually wanted to hear about my short stories and upcoming dance routines. We started hanging out after school, doing everything from study sessions to mini talent shows. They didn't make me choose between being a science geek or a pom-pom enthusiast; they embraced both. No more scanning my words before speaking, no more side-eye over my heritage or "too many clubs." They just accepted all of me.

My old lunch group was puzzled but didn't kick up drama. "I found my crew," I told them, and that was that. Through this experience, I realized the power of the Four Ls:

- Listen to your gut when it tells you you're forcing yourself to fit in.
- Love every part of who you are, sparkly routines and advanced classes included.
- Live your truth boldly, even if it feels risky.
- Lean on people who celebrate all your quirks.

Not every day was perfect, but I finally felt genuinely seen. If anyone out there feels stuck, I hope you find your "island of misfits" too, where you can be every weird and wonderful thing you are.

Case Study: The Artsy Athlete

Marina was known for her talent in basketball. Everyone expected her to train non-stop to go pro. But she secretly loved painting and wanted to take an art class. She used the Four Ls:

- Listen to Her Heart: She acknowledged that painting made her feel alive.
- Love Herself: She reassured herself it was okay to like things off the court.
- Live Her Truth: She signed up for art class, letting people see her creative side.
- Lean on Others: Her coach and teammates ended up being supportive, and her parents encouraged her newfound balance.

Marina realized life isn't one-dimensional, and being authentic meant embracing all her passions.

Quick Quiz Box

Which of the 4 Ls encourages you to be gentle with your mistakes and celebrate who you are?

- A) Listen to My Heart
- B) Love Myself
- C) Live My Truth
- D) Lean on Others

(Answer: B. Loving yourself means accepting imperfections and treating yourself with kindness.)

Journal Reflection Box

Identify a moment when you felt like you were pretending to be someone else. How could the 4 Ls (Listen, Love, Live, Lean) help you show your true self in a similar situation next time?

Action Challenge Chart

Authentic Moment	Four Ls in Action	Outcome / Feeling
Choosing elective classes	Listen to My Heart (pick what excites me)	Energized, more invested
Sharing your real opinion	Love Myself (respecting my own voice)	Felt honest, built real connections
Joining a supportive group	Lean on Others (seek out like-minded friends)	Felt safe to explore new ideas

    A Growth Mindset Ninja understands that being real isn't always easy, but it's worth it. When you Listen to what's inside, Love who you are, Live life based on what matters to you, and Lean on your tribe, you'll find a deeper sense of purpose and belonging. Because life's too short to pretend you're anything less than your amazing, authentic self!

Chapter 10 Key Takeaways

1. Be Real. Authenticity is about aligning actions with your true interests.
2. Four Ls. Listen to your heart, Love yourself, Live your truth, Lean on others.
3. Honesty Builds Deeper Bonds. Real friends appreciate the real you.

Mini-FAQ

Q1: What if my friends don't like the 'real me'?
A: Better to be in a group that loves your genuine self than to fake it. You can still find common ground, but you deserve friends who see your full personality as a plus.

Q2: Is it rude to disagree or say no when I'm being 'true to myself'?
A: Not if you do it respectfully. Authenticity includes respecting others. "No thanks, that's not my style" is honest, but kind, compared to nodding along and feeling miserable.

Finally, with authenticity lighting your path, let's wrap it up with a last spark of inspiration and your next steps onward.

FINAL THOUGHTS

YOUR JOURNEY TO A GROWTH MINDSET

A Note from Me to You

If you've made it all the way here, give yourself a giant high-five (or a celebratory ninja bow, I'll leave the style up to you). You're officially a Growth Mindset Ninja, now!

Putting in the effort to explore new ideas, practice fresh strategies, and occasionally laugh at awkward metaphors means you're already way ahead in this growth mindset game.

There's a part of me that hopes you snorted or giggled at least once while reading (I mean, that's why half the jokes are there). But more importantly, I hope you caught glimpses of your own potential, perhaps in the story of a nervous ninja stepping up to the stage or a perfectionist ninja learning to embrace a messy draft.

Remember that you're the hero of your own story. Each success, stumble, lesson, and do-over is building a you that's stronger, wiser, and surprisingly agile, able to shimmy out of tough situations and leap toward the things that matter.

As you close this book, keep in mind that real life is basically a never-ending training montage. You'll face new challenges, meet new obstacles, and discover new sides of yourself you never knew existed. My hope is that you'll keep these ninja-inspired strategies close, ready to whip them out when self-doubt creeps in or a fresh obstacle leaps in your path.

Thank you for trusting me enough to hang out with these ninjas. Your time is valuable, and the fact that you chose to spend some of it here means a lot. Wherever you go next, may you leap forward with confidence, bounce back from failures with a grin, and, yes, occasionally let out a triumphant I haven't done it, YET!

What You've Learned

Over these chapters, you've discovered ways to:

- ✓ Transform perfectionism into progress, because "done is better than perfect."
- ✓ Adapt and pivot when life's curveballs fly your way.
- ✓ Laugh off embarrassing moments instead of letting them define you.
- ✓ Build unwavering grit and see failures as stepping stones.
- ✓ Harness the magic of "yet," turning self-doubt into self-improvement.
- ✓ Tame shyness, one friendly introduction at a time.
- ✓ Face fears head-on by "looking around, imagining calm, opening up, and being brave."
- ✓ Flow like water when plans change unexpectedly.
- ✓ Stay true to who you are, quirks and all, through authenticity.
- ✓ Replace negativity with trust, treating each relationship like an Emotional Bank Account in which you invest.

These strategies remind you that your mindset, not your circumstances, often determines your success.

Your Next Steps

1. Practice daily. Growth isn't a "once and done" deal; it's built little by little. Keep these ninja strategies handy and use them whenever life tests you.

2. Give yourself grace. Even ninjas stumble. It's okay to struggle or fail. Every slip-up is another chance to learn.
3. Seek support. Friends, family, counselors, they're all part of your "village." Don't be afraid to lean on them for guidance or a pep talk.
4. Reflect often. Look back at where you started. Celebrate your wins, no matter how small, and use setbacks as valuable lessons.

You've Got This!

You're more than the challenges you face. You can shift your perspective, calm your anxieties, and keep moving forward, one fearless step at a time. This book offers you the ninja moves, but the real adventure is yours to shape. Keep showing up, stay open to possibilities, and never forget the power of a growth mindset.

The world needs your unique spark, so let it shine, Ninja!

With love and support,
Mary Nhin

NINJA MOVES GLOSSARY

Perfectionism – F.L.O.W.
- F – Face Your Fear: Pinpoint what scares you about making mistakes and shrink its power by naming it.
- L – Limit Unrealistic Standards: Aim for progress over perfection; give yourself grace to learn.
- O – Observe & Adjust: Treat setbacks like experiments. If one method fails, brainstorm another approach.
- W – Work in Chunks: Tackle big tasks in smaller steps, celebrating every mini-win.

Growth Mindset – The Power of "Yet"
- Add "Yet": Swap "I can't do this" for "I can't do this yet."
- Stretch Yourself: Attempt challenges just outside your comfort zone.
- Learn from Slip-Ups: Every mistake is data guiding you toward improvement.
- Share Your Wins & Struggles: Discussing progress keeps motivation alive.

Embarrassment – S.H.I.N.E.
- Stop & Breathe: Pause the panic with a slow, deep breath.

- Humor: Laugh it off if you can, embarrassment loses its sting when you see the funny side.
- Identify the Lesson: Ask, "What can I learn from this cringe moment?"
- Normalize: Everyone makes mistakes; you're far from alone.
- Embrace the Moment: Own it, let the blush fade, and move forward with confidence.

Flexible Thinking – The Three Ts
- Try Making New Rules: Shake up your routine (or a game!) so your mind stays open to alternatives.
- Tell Jokes: Wordplay boosts creativity and eases rigid thinking.
- Think Out Loud: List every possibility, even silly ones, before settling on a final plan.

Fear – The L.I.O.N. Method
- Look Around: Ground yourself by noticing you're physically safe.
- Imagine a Happy Place: Mentally "teleport" somewhere comforting.
- Open Up: Talk to someone you trust about your fears.
- Now Be Brave: Tackle the fear in baby steps, courage isn't about zero fear, but acting despite it.

Grit – The 4 Cs
- Confident: Visualize success to spark self-belief.
- Calm: Quiet inner chaos with positive mantras like "I can do this."
- Carefree: Challenge worst-case scenarios, realize most stumbles aren't the end of the world.
- Capable: Set goals, practice steadily, and trust your growing skills.

Fury – C.A.L.M.
- C – Count to 10 – Give your brain time to think before reacting.
- A – Allow Yourself to Feel All the Feelings – Say to yourself, I feel upset, and that's okay, but I can control how I respond.

- L – Listen to Your Body – Notice how your body feels and take deep breaths to relax.
- M – Make a Positive Choice – Choose a calm response instead of letting your anger take over.

Adaptability – Flow Like Water
- Observe: Assess the new situation without panicking.
- Stay Fluid: Remain open to shifting plans if obstacles appear.
- Go Around Obstacles: Ask, "How else can I reach my goal?" instead of giving up.
- Embrace Change: Let every plot twist be a chance for growth or creativity.

Negativity – Emotional Bank Accounts
- Recognize: See that every interaction is a deposit (positive) or withdrawal (negative).
- Make Deposits: Compliments, honest apologies, active listening, kept promises.
- Limit Withdrawals: Avoid sarcasm, blaming, or ignoring. Approach problems with kindness.
- Monitor Your Own Account: Talk kindly to yourself too, negativity toward yourself drains self-confidence.

Authenticity – The 4 Ls
- Listen to My Heart: Honor what really speaks to you (interests, values, feelings).
- Love Myself: Practice self-compassion and celebrate your quirks.
- Live My Truth: Let your actions align with who you genuinely are.
- Lean on Others: Seek supportive people who appreciate the real you.

Use this quick-reference guide whenever you need a refresher on how to overcome perfectionism, bend instead of break, handle embarrassment, build grit, unlock your "yet," nudge past shyness, face fears bravely, flow like water through change, live authentically, and steer clear of negativity. Each ninja strategy is a handy tool in your everyday life, mix and match them as you keep leveling up your growth mindset journey!

NINJA MOVES GLOSSARY

HELP AND SUPPORT RESOURCES

If you or someone you know is feeling lost, overwhelmed, or unsure of what to do, know that help is available. Many organizations and individuals are ready to support you.

Please reach out by calling or visiting the resources listed below. If the first attempt doesn't provide the help you need, don't lose hope, keep trying. You are not alone.

For any life-threatening crisis call

CRISIS CALL CENTER (available 24/7)
   1-800-273-8255 or text ANSWER to 839863

Substance Abuse

If you or a friend may be struggling with drug or alcohol use and are unsure what to do, reach out by calling or visiting:
National Council on Alcoholism and Drug Abuse
   1-800-622-2255
   www.ncadd.org

If you're concerned about a family member or friend struggling with alcohol or drug use and don't know how to help, reach out by calling or visiting:

Al-Anon/Alateen
   1-888-425-2666
   www.al-anon.alateen.org

For information about drugs, alcohol, and tobacco, reach out by calling or visiting:

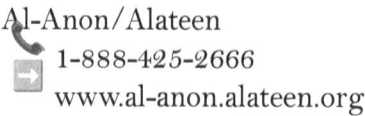
The American Council for Drug Education
   1-888-286-5027
      www.phoenixhouse.org

Partnership for a Drug-Free America
📞 1-855-DRUGFREE
➡️ www.drugfree.org

Eating Disorders

If you or a friend may be experiencing anorexia, bulimia, or an overeating disorder and need support, reach out by calling or visiting:

National Eating Disorders Association
📞 1-800-931-2237
➡️ www.nationaleatingdisorders.org

Physical and Mental Health

If you or a friend are considering suicide, PLEASE call the Crisis Call Center or visit:

Suicide Hotline
📞 1-800-273-TALK
➡️ www.afsp.org

For more information about depression or mental illnesses, creach out by calling or visiting:

National Institute of Mental Health Information Center
📞 1-866-615-6464
➡️ www.nimh.nih.gov

If you or your friends are concerned about contracting or having an STD or AIDS, reach out by calling or visiting:

Sexually Transmitted Diseases
📞 1-800-227-8929
➡️ www.cdc.gov/STD

National AIDS Hotline
📞 1-800-232-4636
➡️ www.cdcnpin.org/hiv/

Grief and Loss

If you or a friend are struggling with a tragedy or the loss of a loved one and don't know how to cope, reach out by calling or visiting:

Tragedy Assistance Program for Survivors
   📞 1-800-959-8277
   ➡️ www.taps.org

Teen Pregnancy

If you are pregnant or worried about becoming pregnant and need more information about your options, reach out by calling or visiting:

American Pregnancy Helpline
   📞 1-866-942-6466
   ➡️ www.thehelpline.org

Birthright International
   📞 1-800-550-4900
   ➡️ www.birthright.org

If you have a baby now or are having a baby, reach out by calling or visiting:

Baby Your Baby
   📞 1-800-826-9662
   ➡️ www.babyyourbaby.org

Abuse

If you are in a dating relationship with an abusive person, reach out by calling or visiting:

National Teen Dating Abuse Helpline
   📞 1-866-331-9474
   ➡️ www.loveisrespect.org

If you or a friend, male or female, are a victim of rape, incest, or any form of sexual abuse, reach out by calling or visiting:

Rape, Abuse, and Incest National Network
  1-800-656-4673
  www.rainn.org

If you or a friend or any family member is being abused at home, reach out by calling or visiting:

National Domestic Violence Hotline
  1-800-799-7233
  www.ndvh.org

If you or a friend is being bullied, creach out by calling or visiting:

Speak Up: School Violence and Bullying
  1-866-773-2587
  www.cpyv.org

If you or a friend is being cyberbullied, visit:
  www.stopbullying.gov/cyberbullying/

Or call: Cyber Tipline
  1-800-843-5678
  www.cybertipline.com

Gang Prevention

Boys and Girls Club of America
Find a club near you:
  www.bgca.org

Education

If you're worried about how to pay for college or future career training, reach out by calling or visiting:

Educational Funding
📞 1-800-USA-LEARN / 1-800-725-3276
➡ www.ed.gov

Federal Student Aid
📞 1-800-4-FED AID / 1-800-433-3243
➡ www.fafsa.ed.gov

If you want to learn how to handle money wisely or save for your future, visit:
➡ www.mymoney.gov

Volunteerism

If you and your friends are interested in making a difference and learning leadership skills at the same time, reach out by calling or visiting:

YMCA
📞 1-800-872-9622
➡ www.ymca.net

America's Charities
📞 1-800-458-9505
➡ www.charities.org

United Way
Find United Way in your community:
➡ www.unitedway.org

General Youth Support Services

If you're a runaway and need help or want to return home, reach out by calling or visiting:

National Runaway Safeline
📞 1-800-RUNAWAY
➡ www.1800runaway.org

If you're homeless and need somewhere to stay, food to eat, and crisis care, reach out by calling or visiting:

Covenant House Nine-Line
 1-800-999-9999
 www.covenanthouse.org

If you think you may have a problem with online gaming addiction, reach out by calling or visiting:

On-Line Gamers Anonymous
 www.olganon.org

If you need help working something out or just need to talk to someone, reach out by calling or visiting:

Teen Line
 1-800-TLC-TEEN
 https://teenlineonline.org/talk-now
Or text 'teen' to 839863

BOOKS & RESOURCES MENTIONED IN THIS BOOK

Mindset: The New Psychology of Success by Carol S. Dweck
A classic look at how a growth mindset helps you view challenges as opportunities. Dweck's research underscores the power of believing you can improve through effort, practice, and learning from mistakes.

Grit: The Power of Passion and Perseverance by Angela Duckworth
Explores how sticking with your goals over the long term often matters more than sheer talent. Duckworth offers practical tips for nurturing your own "grit muscle."

The 7 Habits of Highly Effective Teens by Sean Covey
A teen-focused adaptation of the famous 7 Habits framework. Covey's straightforward approach provides actionable habits for school success, personal growth, and leadership.

Atomic Habits by James Clear
Shows you how small, consistent actions can lead to major life changes, perfect for anyone wanting to improve study habits, fitness goals, or daily routines in a manageable way.

The Mindful Teen by Dzung X. Vo, MD
A practical guide to mindfulness techniques specifically geared toward teens. Learn how to reduce stress, manage emotions, and navigate relationships with more awareness.

Don't Sweat the Small Stuff for Teens by Richard Carlson
Offers simple strategies to help teens keep life's inevitable bumps in perspective, build resilience, and maintain a calm mindset in the face of everyday stressors.

Brainstorm: The Power and Purpose of the Teenage Brain by Daniel J. Siegel, MD
> Explains the science behind the teenage brain and how to harness its natural creativity, exploration, and adaptability during these transformative years.

Apps & Websites

Headspace or Calm (Meditation & Mindfulness)
> Guided meditations and breathing exercises that help you build calm into your everyday life. Perfect for mental breaks between classes or before a big exam.

Quizlet (Study & Memorization)
> A handy app for creating flashcards, quizzes, and study games, especially useful for staying organized and reducing last-minute cramming.

TED Talks (Inspiration & Learning)
> A wide range of short, engaging talks by thought leaders on personal growth, creativity, and leadership. Great for a quick boost of motivation.

Habitica or Done (Habit Tracking)
> Turn your goals into mini challenges or "quests" to stay motivated. Especially useful for tracking study routines, exercise, or any new habit you want to form.

YouVersion Bible App / Daily Quote Apps / Motivational Quote of the Day
> If you enjoy daily doses of inspiration, there are plenty of apps that share uplifting quotes or spiritual insights to keep you centered.

Khan Academy (Academic Support)
> Offers free lessons in math, science, and more, ideal for supplementing what you learn in school or catching up on tricky topics.

Other Products by Mary Nhin

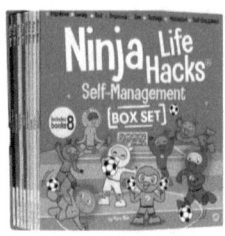

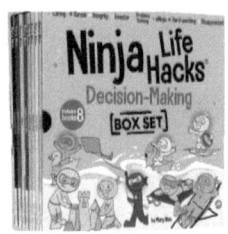

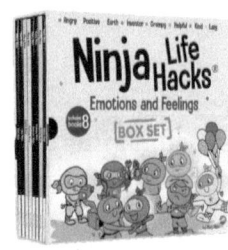
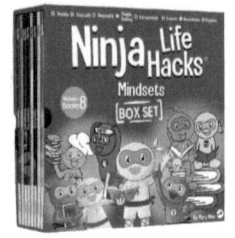

NinjaLifeHacks.tv

About the Author

Mary Nhin is a social impact entrepreneur and author of the flagship series, Ninja Life Hacks, a social-emotional learning brand, with 124 books and 99 characters, dedicated to empowering children with life skills. It's captured the hearts of over four million readers and continues to lead the way for an exciting adventure in social, emotional learning.

At the core of Mary Nhin's writing is a flicker of hope. While the writer frequently lays her soul bare, tackling issues such as failures, acceptance, and loneliness, there's always a silver lining. That's particularly true of her book series, "Ninja Life Hacks," which looks at failures as a transformative experience.

Under Mary's leadership, the Ninja Life Hacks brand of books, resources, and toys have empowered people worldwide with social, emotional coping strategies to use for a lifetime. Her books have been translated in twelve countries.

As Co-founder and Chief Creative Officer of Nhinja Sushi, the mom and pop restaurant has blossomed into a five location restaurant chain, serving up high quality sushi and freshly cooked meals to busy families. Today, over 1500+ people visit Nhinja locations daily.

Mary's visionary leadership earned her and her teams a collection of industry accolades including: Woman of Integrity Award Winner (Better Business Bureau), Most Admired CEO (The Journal Record), HER award (405 Magazine), Top 50 Most Influential Oklahomans Power List (Journal Record), Top 100

Small Businesses (U.S. Chamber of Commerce), AAPI Strong Restaurant Winner (National ACE), In the Lead Female Leader (Journal Record), 40 Under Forty (OKC Business), Inc 5000 (Inc. Magazine), Best Sushi (Edmond Life and Leisure and Edmond Sun), Best Finance Books For Kids (Investopedia), Best Kids Money Books (Mom.com).

    She and her husband, Kang Nhin, are proud parents of three children, Mikey, Kobe, and Jojo.

WEBSITE: www.ninjalifehacks.tv

WEBSITE: www.nhinja.com

LINKEDIN: @Marynhin

FB: Nhinja Sushi

FB: Ninja Life Hacks

IG: @nhinjasushi

IG: @officialninjalifehacks

TT: @officialninjalifehacks

YT: youtube.com/@NinjaLifeHacks

X: @nhinjas

Email: mary@ninjalifehacks.tv

www.ingramcontent.com/pod-product-compliance
Lightning Source LLC
La Vergne TN
LVHW091543070526
838199LV00002B/191